Connections
Quadrant II Time Management

A. Roger Merrill
with
Rebecca R. Merrill

Foreword by
Stephen R. Covey

The Institute for Principle-Centered Leadership

Connections
Quadrant II Time Management

Revised 1989—2nd Printing 1990

Original copyright © 1987 by
The Institute for Principle-Centered Leadership
Originally published in 1987 for use with
Personal Leadership Seminars
Revised for general distribution in this new edition

Library of Congress Catalog Card Number
89-080383
ISBN 0-9622363-0-6

Lithographed in the United States of America
Publishers Press
Salt Lake City, Utah

Acknowledgments

To the many who have influenced my thinking over more than 20 years of focused pursuit of effective personal management...

Thank you.

To Dr. Stephen R. Covey, who has influenced and helped shape my thinking on this and many other subjects...

Thank you.

To my co-workers at the Institute for Principle-Centered Leadership and the Covey Leadership Center, who have helped in many ways conceptually and with production...

Thank you.

To my family, who has consciously sacrificed time for this effort and has been understanding and supportive...

Thank you.

Most of all, to Rebecca, my wife, who has really been a co-author in thought, design and writing...To you and what we share is this work dedicated...

Thank you.

Ariel Roger Merrill

Foreword

I first met Roger Merrill 26 years ago when he was a student of mine in Organizational Behavior at Brigham Young University. Some years later, by coincidence, our paths crossed again. I happened to see Roger as he was presenting on the subject, "The Principle of Principles."

As I slipped into the back of the room and listened to his presentation, I soon learned that we still shared a common interest in leadership and life management based on a set of proven principles. We have since become even better friends and full-time professional associates as Roger has joined us as vice president of the Covey Leadership Center.

PRINCIPLE-CENTERED LIVING

I am firmly convinced of the value of principle-centered living and leadership. For many years, I have taught the "Seven Habits of Highly Effective People", which are the integration of principles of personal and interpersonal effectiveness.

In **Connections,** Roger focuses primarily on the principles on which the first three habits—the habits of Private Victory—are based. These habits include **proactivity**—recognizing and accepting our ability to act based on our values, rather than reacting based on emotion or circumstance; **beginning with the end in mind**—creating mentally first what we want to create in reality; and **putting first things first**—using our proactivity to transform mental creation into realization through subordination of less important things to those of greater value.

Roger provides a practical process that incorporates these habits of Private Victory and helps people to translate their values into daily living. Having the "right connections," he says, is the key to balance, peace, productivity and even to effective relationships with others. It's the same inside-out approach to effectiveness contained in the "Seven Habits".

The idea of principle-centered living consistently strikes a responsive chord with people who struggle daily to achieve a healthy balance between the demand for production—for bottom-line results—and the need for periodic maintenance and self-development. Once caught in the activity trap—where attention is paid to the things that are pressing, popular, proximate, pleasant, and pleasing—it's hard to escape.

People begin to feel disconnected, disjointed, out of touch with themselves, enslaved, powerless and consumed by crises, which seem to come one after another like the pounding surf. Controlled by the tyranny of the "urgent," they do less and less of the "important" and often begin to sacrifice personal and family goals to meet the demands of their jobs.

THREE GENERATIONS OF TIME MANAGEMENT

When people turn to experts in the field of "time management" for help, they find the accumulated benefits of three generations of theory and implementation.

The first generation, characterized by notes and checklists, gives recognition and inclusiveness to the many demands on our time. The second generation, characterized by calendars and appointment books, reflects an effort to look ahead and schedule future events and activities. The third generation—the current field—focuses on daily planning and adds the important ideas of clarifying values, prioritizing and goal setting.

But even with the tremendous progress represented by this evolution, people continue to feel frustrated and victimized. They continue to respond—albeit more efficiently—to the "urgent" instead of the "important." The "efficiency" focus enables them to get more things done in less time—but often at the expense of relationships, spontaneity and personal peace and happiness. Prioritized schedules make good servants but bad masters.

As a long-time student in the field of time management, I have attended literally dozens of seminars on the subject, and I have found something of value in each, but I have never been completely satisfied.

THE FOURTH GENERATION

I am personally convinced that a new generation is beginning to emerge, and that this generation is different in kind from the three that have preceded it.

Rather than focusing on *efficiency*, it focuses on *effectiveness*. Instead of *time* and *things*, it emphasizes *relationships* and *results*. More, really, than "time management," it's "personal leadership." It's life balance.

And **Connections** is on the crest of the wave of this new generation. While some time management courses help people identify values and priorities, they leave them without a process for connecting those values to their daily lives in a balanced way. The tools they provide—the third generation planners—focus on daily planning and therefore keep people in an urgency-reactive mode, failing to facilitate a lifestyle focused on relationships and results. Consequently, people get lost in the gap between principle and practice.

In this powerful little book, Roger shows people how to close the gap, how to become congruent, how to walk their talk. Rather than prescribing specific practices, the book empowers people to live their lives in harmony with values and principles.

While Roger and I have similar interests, our minds work differently. While I focus on principle, Roger comes up with application. One outcome of that synergy is the Seven Habits Organizer, a tool that facilitates a fourth generation lifestyle by subordinating schedules to people and by helping individuals organize their lives around their mission, roles and goals through a 15 to 30 minute weekly process.

I highly recommend Roger's book to all who want a closer *connection* between their deepest beliefs and their daily behaviors. I can promise readers that they will improve their personal effectiveness and enrich their personal relationships as they commit to principle-centered leadership and life management.

Stephen R. Covey

Contents

Connections
Quadrant II Time Management

CHAPTER

Where in the Universe is Quadrant II?

I woke up this morning and looked out my window to discover that the unbelievable had happened...it had actually snowed! After two and a half months of atypical, practically snowless Utah weather (with the ski resort owners in the final stages of delirium), the prayed-for precipitation was making its way lazily through the atmosphere and turning the world white with possibility.

It was also turning my own world upside down. I had planned to get up early and write. I **wanted** to write. I was excited about working on something I felt was deeply important. But that beautiful snow suddenly created another want...and the thought of spending a Saturday sailing down the slopes with the light spray of fresh powder on my face was almost overwhelming.

I felt other wants, too...part of me wanted to go to a family birthday party we had planned during the day; part of me wanted to cloister myself in my study and completely isolate myself all day to write. And there was that ever-present temptation to simply turn over and go back to sleep.

And then, of course, there were the **shoulds**. I knew I **should** get out of bed. I knew I really **should** work on the book. And, if I let myself think about it, there were probably a hundred and one things on a **should** list somewhere in my cerebrum that were clamoring for my attention.

As I considered the possibilities, I realized that this was an ideal example of what I wanted to write about: so many influences creating **want to do's**, so many factors creating **should do's**, and the changing ability of the individual **to do**.

Now most people equate "time management" with "getting more things done in less time." That's fine, provided the things you **want** to do, the things you feel you **should** do, and the things you actually **do** are all the same. But for most of us, there is an uncomfortable conflict between the three that is unresolved by simply **doing more things**, no matter how efficiently we may do them.

I believe that as well as doing things right, truly effective time management is **doing the right things**— the things you really want to do. More than "time management" in the traditional sense, it's **personal leadership**. It's having a deep harmony between the wants and shoulds in life and having increasing power to do. It is the connection of what you do in any given moment of your life to what you are, what you believe, what you deeply value.

It sounds easy enough: find out what you really want to do and go do it. But if it were that simple, most of us wouldn't be frustrated, feeling rushed and behind, wishing we had more spontaneity in our lives and feeling in varying degrees controlled by circumstances or the expectations of others.

The fact is that a day of life is not the automatic incarnation of a planning page, no matter how well that page is written. Forces are acting on us constantly that influence what we want to do, what we feel we should do and what we can, in fact, do. To ignore those forces (were it even possible) might be to live without interruption, but it would also be to live without opportunity, spontaneity, and the rich moments of which "life" is made.

We are constantly faced with the challenge of navigating effectively through a myriad of currents, some of which appear unexpectedly, some of which we don't even recognize, many of which are not under our immediate control, and all of which create desires within us or expectations of us to which we must respond in some meaningful way. It is the premise of this book that the empowering principles that enable us to navigate successfully, to manage our time to do what we really want to do, are found in that marvelous part of the universe known as "Quadrant II."

We actually spend our time in one of four ways, as diagrammed on the following time management matrix.

The Time Management Matrix

	Urgent	**Not Urgent**
Important	**I** ACTIVITIES • Crises • Pressing problems • Deadline-driven projects	**II** ACTIVITIES • Preparation • Crisis prevention • Values clarification • Planning • Relationship building • True re-creation
Not Important	**III** ACTIVITIES • Interruptions, some phone calls • Some Mail, some reports • Some meetings • Many proximate, pressing matters • Many popular activities	**IV** ACTIVITIES • Trivia, busy work • Junk mail • Some phone calls • Time wasters • "Escape" activities

Quadrant I represents those things that are pressing and proximate, the "urgent and important." Included here might be such activities as handling an irate client, meeting a deadline, repairing a broken-down machine or having heart surgery. Some Quadrant I activities are Quadrant I by nature, but many surface here through time mismanagement problems. This is the Quadrant of Crisis.

Quadrant II includes activities that are "important, but not urgent." This is the Quadrant of Quality. Increasing time spent here increases our connecting power and our ability to do. This area contains activities such as long-range planning, preventive maintenance, acquiring knowledge and skills, and investing in relationships and networks through deep, honest listening.

Quadrant III, including "urgent, but not important" activities, is almost the phantom of Quadrant I. Urgency creates the illusion of importance, but the actual activities, if they are important at all, are important to someone else. Many phone calls, meetings and drop-in visitors fall into this category. We spend time in Quadrant III meeting other people's priorities and expectations more often than we'd like to admit, thinking we're really in Quadrant I.

And Quadrant IV is reserved for those activities that are "not urgent and not important." Of course, we really shouldn't be there at all. But many of us get so battle-scarred being tossed to and fro in Quadrants I and III that we escape to Quadrant IV for survival. What kinds of things are in Quadrant IV? Not necessarily recreational things, because recreation in the sense of re-creation is a valuable activity and would more likely be found in Quadrant II. But reading addictive light novels, habitually watching "mindless" television shows, or engaging in prolonged unconstructive talk or gossip around the water fountain at the office would qualify as Quadrant IV time wasters.

Many of us spend the large majority of our time in Quadrants I and III, frequently wishing we were in Quadrant IV. We become victims of the tyranny of the urgent, conditioned to respond to anything that has **"now!"** attached to it.

We begin to use urgency as a motivator of self and others, creating a lifestyle based on the "cry wolf!" syndrome. "I have to do this **now!**" "This is **urgent!**" And we run, time after time, only to discover when we arrive, that we're exhausted, our creativity is shot, and the wolf often isn't really there after all.

So we wear ourselves out, we become reactive, we get cynical about ourselves and we finally reach the point where we say, "What does it matter? I'm rushing around, and I'm not even doing what I really want to do. I just don't feel good about my life."

If we have a role in leadership or management, we tend to transfer the same style to our interpersonal activities. We attempt to create unity around a project by crying "urgent!" and other people run. But after a time, they get tired of running, too. They become increasingly cynical and pessimistic and develop their own pace—a reactionary pace—so that when a true emergency does come along, it's very difficult to create a unified, effective effort.

When we turn to the current field of "time management" for answers to our frustration, we generally find tools to help us prioritize our urgent Quadrant I and III activities and do them more efficiently—so that we can do more of them.

But take just a moment and ask yourself this question: **Is there anything in my personal or professional life that is not urgent, but which, if I did every week for 52 weeks, would significantly impact my effectiveness?**

I believe there is. I believe you'll find it in Quadrant II. And I believe, if you think deeply about it, you'll really **want** to do it. You'll feel it's something you really **should** do. How you **can** do it, and how you can do whatever else you really want to do, is what this book is about.

CHAPTER

And Where in the World Are You?

In order to get where you want to go, you have to start out from where you are. If moving into Quadrant II is your objective, you first need to determine where you are now in terms of your own Quadrant II time management capability.

You were probably able to get some idea of which quadrants most of your activities fit into when we described them in Chapter One. But let's look at it from another perspective.

Before going any further, take a pencil and fill out the following questionnaire. Strengths and weaknesses in each of ten areas are briefly described by four sets of statements reflecting related attitudes, skills or practices. As you read each set of statements, check the number on the continuum between the statements that most accurately describes you. Use "0" if the statement on the left represents you exactly; use "5" if you feel you are perfectly described by the statement on the right. Numbers "1" through "4" reflect the various positions between the two extremes.

Example

SECTION ONE

1. I often feel frustrated, wondering if I am doing what I really want to do day after day.

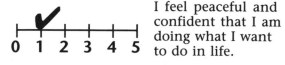

I feel peaceful and confident that I am doing what I want to do in life.

These questions are designed to increase your self-awareness in specific areas that will be explained later.

QUADRANT II

TIME MANAGEMENT EVALUATION

SECTION ONE

1. I often feel frustrated, wondering if I am doing what I really want to do day after day.

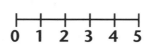

I feel peaceful and confident that I am doing what I want to do in life.

2. My life is very busy, but I often wonder how much of what I am doing really counts.

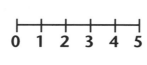

I feel the things I do every day are meaningful and contribute to my overall goals in life.

3. If someone were to ask me for a written copy of my lifetime goals, I could not provide it.

I have thought deeply about the meaning of life, and have established a written set of personal goals and values.

4. I sometimes get glimpses of what I should do with my life, but they somehow get lost in the busy activity of my days.

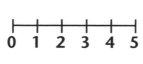

I frequently review my directions in life and keep them constantly before me.

Section One Total

SECTION TWO

1. It is often hard for me to decide which of many things is important to do.

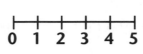

I can quickly decide what is most important for me to do.

2. I am easily frustrated by changes in plans.

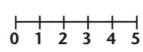

I can handle changes peacefully and confidently.

3. I usually say "yes" when anyone asks me to do something, and I feel guilty if I want to say "no."

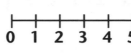

I politely tell people "no" from time to time if I feel I cannot give a request the time and effort it deserves. I do not feel guilty when doing this.

4. I nearly always feel "buried," having more to do than I can possibly handle.

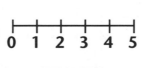

I feel comfortable about the pace and progress of life.

Section Two Total

SECTION THREE

1. I feel that other people and circumstances control a good part of my life.

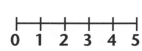

I feel in charge of my life most of the time.

2. I feel worried and anxious much of the time.

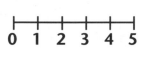

I generally have a positive attitude about my life and challenges.

3. I often find myself apologizing to others for losing control and reacting too quickly.

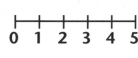

I am usually in control of my actions and feelings, even in highly charged emotional situations and difficult circumstances.

4. I often lose my enthusiasm for projects or goals before they are complete, or I find myself becoming frustrated if a challenge keeps going on and on.

I am able to see things through to their completion, and I can keep my goals in sight through challenges that last months or even years.

Section Three Total

SECTION FOUR

1. I usually find I have to spend much of the time I have planned for a project in locating the right tools and materials to do the job.

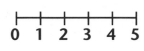

I plan ahead and organize necessary tools and materials in advance so that I can spend allocated time directly on a project.

2. When I try to involve others in a project, I usually meet with resistance, conflicting schedules and lack of support.

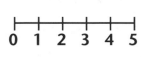

I communicate with others in advance when I need their help with a project and I involve them directly in the planning and scheduling process.

3. When I have a project to do, I take a sizeable amount of time and attack it with gusto.

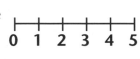

When I have a project to do, I analyze it and break it down into component parts, setting aside several smaller time blocks for necessary planning and preparation.

4. My day's activities are often interrupted by commitments I have forgotten or by unanticipated time demands from others.

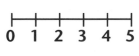

I practice personal planning on a regular basis and involve my family and/or business associates in weekly planning to coordinate schedules and goals.

Section Four Total

SECTION FIVE

1. I frequently have to apologize for being a little late or missing appointments.

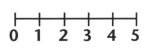

I am punctual and consistent in keeping appointments with others.

2. I often disappoint friends or family members by failing to keep an appointment or fulfill a commitment to them.

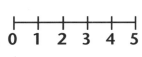

A commitment to a friend or member of my family receives the same priority as a commitment to a business associate or other acquaintance.

3. I frequently excuse myself for not fulfilling a commitment I have made to myself or achieving a personal goal.

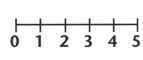

I honor commitments of time and resources to myself as well as to others.

4. I frequently make more commitments than I can really handle well.

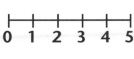

I limit my commitments to those I am relatively certain I can handle.

Section Five Total

SECTION SIX

1. I consistently plan to do more than I actually get done, and I feel like I'm always behind.

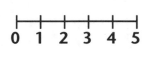

I am generally able to accomplish what I plan to do within the time and re-sources allocated, and to mentally and emotionally "let go" of other things.

2. I frequently underestimate how long things will take.

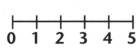

My estimate of how long projects and appointments will take is usually realistic.

3. I often work frantically up to the last minute to complete a project and feel disap-pointed in the quality of the results.

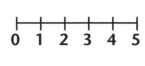

I tend to work on projects at an organized, steady pace and complete quality work on schedule.

4. I tend to view projects, goals and challenges as huge mountains that have to be climbed.

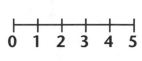

I perceive projects, goals and chal-lenges in terms of small component parts to be accom-plished one at a time.

Section Six Total

SECTION SEVEN

1. My days are filled with "interruptions" that keep me from being as effective as I could be.

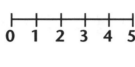

I am able to set aside specific blocks of time on a regular basis to accomplish goals without interruption.

2. At any one moment, I am usually distracted by a number of different things running through my mind.

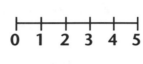

At any one moment, I concentrate fully on the experience at hand and enjoy what I am doing.

3. When I try to meet with an individual, our time together is often interrupted by phone calls or other people.

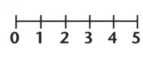

When I meet with an individual, that person has my undivided attention.

4. I work on a task for long hours at a time and feel tired and ineffective.

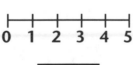

I divide my time into short productive segments and change tasks frequently.

Section Seven Total

SECTION EIGHT

1. I am simply too busy to take time for personal development.

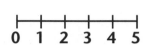

I regularly invest time and effort in personal development.

2. I feel that "personal" time is selfish.

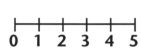

I feel an investment in my own development will help me to be more effective as an employee, spouse, parent, civic leader, or community volunteer.

3. I feel overwhelmed and immobilized by all the things I feel I should do to improve.

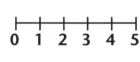

I view improvement as a life-long process and I feel confident in my ability to integrate improvement into my lifestyle at a regular and peaceful pace.

4. I do some things for myself, but I don't feel really "fulfilled" or "complete" as a person.

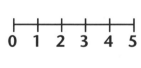

I work to develop the "whole" person and set improvement goals in a wide range of areas.

Section Eight Total

SECTION NINE

1. I feel like the time it takes to communicate with other people keeps me from accomplishing my goals and objectives in life.

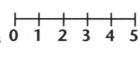

I deeply value others, and want to understand their concerns and views, especially when they differ from mine.

2. I sometimes have to tell people what I want them to do several times before they do it.

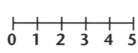

I usually "check understanding" when I communicate with others and misunderstandings are caught early.

3. I often wonder if people really mean what they say to me.

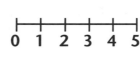

I earnestly try to understand the message being communicated by others, both verbally and through means other than words.

4. When I have interpersonal conflicts, I tend to get frustrated and blame others.

When disagreements occur, I assume there has been a miscommunication and work to remedy the situation.

Section Nine Total

SECTION TEN

1. I sometimes lose track of important information, but I know that piece of paper I put it on is SOMEWHERE!

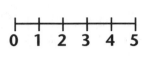

I have an organized method of keeping track of information.

2. I have never used a personal planner, or I have tried to use different planners, but I just can't seem to make them work.

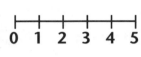

I have a personal organizer that works effectively for me.

3. I have trouble trying to keep track of different areas of my life...home, office, church, etc., all at once.

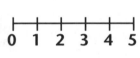

I keep track of my various responsibilities effectively.

4. I often wonder if there is something I'm forgetting, or if I'm spending my time on the most important things.

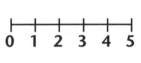

I have an orderly way to keep track of things I want to do and feel comfortable and on target most of the time.

Section Ten Total

Now go back and total your score in each section. Record the figure in the box provided.

Example

SECTION ONE

1. I often feel frustrated, wondering if I am doing what I really want to do day after day.

0 1 2 3 4 5

I feel peaceful and confident that I am doing what I want to do in life.

2. My life is very busy, but I often wonder how much of what I am doing really counts.

0 1 2 3 4 5

I feel the things I do every day are meaningful and contribute to my overall goals in life.

3. If someone were to ask me for a written copy of my lifetime goals, I could not provide it.

0 1 2 3 4 5

I have thought deeply about the meaning of life, and have established a written set of personal goals and values.

4. I sometimes get glimpses of what I should do with my life, but they somehow get lost in the busy activity of my days.

0 1 2 3 4 5

I frequently review my directions in life and keep them constantly before me.

Section One Total

```
9
```

This questionnaire is based on ten characteristics shown by research to be evidenced in the lives of highly effective Quadrant II time managers. Models of success were defined as individuals who:

1. **Were unusually productive**
   This was defined in terms of quality as well as quantity. Those who were selected as models did what they did very well. Excellence was an easily recognizable hallmark of their productivity.

2. **Reflected values compatible with time-proven principles**
   Foremost among the principles reflected were INTEGRITY, CONTRIBUTION, and BALANCE. Individuals who excelled in one area at the expense of family, friends, or effective resource management did not meet the criteria.

3. **Were reasonably calm and happy**
   Calmness and happiness were recognized as the result of a life congruent with inner values. Of course, some stress is a natural part of any life. But no amount of productivity compensated for a life filled with tension, anxiety and unhappiness.

Interestingly, it was only after the research was completed that the dramatic correlation between these criteria and Quadrant II activities was realized.

To enable you to determine where you are in each of these areas, I have listed the characteristics on the following page and provided space for you to record your score. The highest possible score in each area is 20. Your scores on these various factors provide you with a profile of how you see your relative strengths and weakness in each of these areas.

EFFECTIVE QUADRANT II TIME MANAGERS:

1. Keep their values clearly in mind

   Section One Total

2. Evaluate and limit activities and commitments based on fundamental values

   Section Two Total

3. Free themselves to act rather than being acted upon

   Section Three Total

4. Think ahead, prepare and organize

   Section Four Total

5. Honor commitments to self and others

   Section Five Total

6. Accurately determine the achievable

   Section Six Total

7. Focus efforts and energy

   Section Seven Total

8. Continually increase personal capacity

Section Eight Total

9. Are sensitive to others and communicate effectively

Section Nine Total

10. Carefully select and use a few personalized tools

Section Ten Total

It will be helpful for you to go back now and write each factor in the space provided by the section heading on the questionnaire.

Example

SECTION ONE - *Keep values clearly in mind*

1. I often feel frustrated, wondering if I am doing what I really want to do day after day.

0 1 2 3 4 5

I feel peaceful and confident that I am doing what I want to do in life.

In the following chapters, I will be presenting the principles and strategies that will empower you to develop these characteristics in your life and to take up residence in Quadrant II.

CHAPTER

3

How to "Connect" with *Connections*

It was Friday morning. People were filing into the room in various states of awareness. Some were involved in light conversation, some were shuffling through papers or looking for pens, a couple were yawning, and one man was even sitting in the back of the room with his head back and his eyes closed. I figured he must have been in deep contemplation of the mysteries of the universe.

As I began the seminar, the first thing I did was to inform those present that arrangements had been made for two randomly selected participants to go before the Corporate Executive Committee on Monday morning and present a 15 minute summary of this seminar and the benefits they gained from it to that august body. The effect of that announcement was phenomenal. Eyes opened, people sat up, notebooks were opened and pens were poised. Suddenly what I was about to say took on a whole new dimension. The material I was about to present no longer represented an isolated learning experience; it was somehow connected to what was important to them...their careers, their futures, the opportunity to see and be seen by that elite group of powerful decision makers usually hidden behind a mahogany wall. The basic attitude in that room had changed, and I knew from experience that the posture of learning I saw before me would continue throughout the day. The questions would be deep, the effort to understand intense. Knowing that they had to be able to teach what they were being taught created a high priority around learning.

Learning how to learn is a powerful Quadrant II activity. In some respects, it really should be included in Chapter Nine of this book along with other high-leverage Quadrant II activities. But I know that you will get a lot more out of this book if you understand the concept now. So I want to give you the ideas and strategies to help you "connect" with *Connections*.

PREPARE NOW TO TEACH THIS MATERIAL TO SOMEONE ELSE

The participants in the seminar I mentioned left that day with something a lot more meaningful than an eight hour program behind them. They had something **within** them that they were now prepared to share with someone else. In fact, all of the participants did have the opportunity to teach the material the next week to those they supervised, sharing some powerful ideas with others and reinforcing those ideas in their own minds.

The strategy of what we call "three-person teaching" is so fundamental to effective learning that we have adopted it as one of the basic strategies for corporate change at the Covey Leadership Center and the Institute for Principle-Centered Leadership.

I suggest that you learn this material as a potential teacher and that you **determine right now when you are going to teach it and to whom.** I guarantee you will process the information in this book in a much deeper way if you do. Your rate of understanding and your ability to apply the principles taught in this book will be greatly increased.

As an added benefit, you will transform your environment from a restraining to a supportive one as you attempt to effect change in your own life. Let me explain.

We tend to categorize people. When they behave in ways we have come to expect, we feel comfortable around them. Change makes us nervous, and in subtle ways, we resist change in others, often subconsciously.

As you implement change in your own life, you will be faced with an environment of friends and associates who subconsciously resist that change. By sharing with them and teaching them, you will increase their awareness and understanding, and you will find them much more inclined to support your effort to change. As you share what you are learning, how you feel about it and what you are going to do about it, you involve other people. And involvement breeds commitment.

I strongly suggest that you decide now when you are going to teach this information and to whom.

BUILD A FRAMEWORK OF INTEREST

Basically the way we learn is through associative networks. Your brain is constantly receiving data from your sensory experience which is recorded and related to other data being received simultaneously as well as to data previously entered. At any given moment, your brain is recording what you hear, smell, see, feel, and taste, as well as the feelings and emotions you have about it, and is connecting that to the information already stored.

For example, you may walk past a bakery and catch a whiff of freshly baked bread. Suddenly, as clearly as if it were yesterday, you remember your own mother baking bread. You remember how the bread smelled, how it tasted warm with butter melting on top. You remember what your mother looked like, what the kitchen looked like, maybe even whether the day was rainy or sunny or warm. You remember the sound of your mother's voice and the feel of a small piece of the sticky dough in your hands. You even remember the feelings of security, of belonging and comfort you had at the time.

All these associations are wrapped up in that one instant of recorded time. As you process that instant, you also connect it to other instants...perhaps to a much later moment when you were lonely or afraid and you felt the loss of that security you once enjoyed; perhaps to the moment this morning when you buttered your toast; perhaps to a time in your life when you were trying to lose weight and you renounced bread altogether.

The idea is that learning is not an isolated experience. It is, by nature, associative. The more associations you can build around any learning experience, the more powerfully that learning will be ingrained in your mind, and the more readily you will be able to recall and apply that learning at will.

Interest drives learning, and one of the most powerful associations you can create for learning is a mental framework of interest. Before you even approach a subject, you can formulate questions that create something akin to slots in your mind where the information can go with meaning. The process could be compared to the way a computer program formats a disk into sectors for storage and retrieval of information.

You are evidently interested in effective time management. What is it you want to accomplish by reading this book? What are the problems, the concerns, the frustrations you have about the way you manage your time now? Perhaps some of the questions in the previous chapter touched areas of concern in you life. What are they? What is it you want to know or be able to do?

As you ask questions, try to word them in a way that will associate them with your deepest feelings so that they become "burning" questions with far more power to ignite your understanding than a cold, academic query.

Let me show you what a "burning" question is. Suppose it's Saturday morning and you want to get the lawn mowed so you can go play golf with some friends at 9:00. You get the mower out of the garage and try to start it. It won't start. You check the gasoline, look over the engine and try again. It still won't start. You review everything you know about gasoline engines. You go over every step in the process trying to locate the problem. And it still won't start. By now you're getting pretty teed off (which may be as close as you come to your round of golf if you can't get that lawnmower going). **WHAT IS THE PROBLEM?** Now that is a "burning" question.

Now suppose a neighbor, who is an expert mechanic, observes your predicament and walks over to see how he can help. After looking at it for a minute, he points out the one thing you missed, the one bit of information you didn't have, that causes the mower to start right up. Are you ever going to forget it?

Our minds become almost photographic when what we learn is:

1. based on a felt need.
2. associated with values we feel deeply about.
3. tied into an existing framework of knowledge.

So we can get these conditions working for us. We can create the need by examining our own lives and asking questions. We can make those questions burning questions, attaching some feeling and emotion to them. And we can constantly be constructing frameworks of knowledge and interest, creating places for new information to go.

Some people are caught up in the myth that the mind is like a jar. If you fill up the jar, you can't put any more in until you take something out. So you have to limit what you put into the jar.

On the contrary, the more you learn, the more you can learn; the more you have to associate new learning with. The small percentage of brain potential that even the most recognized intellectuals have used gives almost infinite possibility to what the mind can hold. In fact, recent research indicates that our memory capacity may indeed be infinite.

So out of whatever needs, frustrations or desires you may have, ask your burning questions about time management. Create a place for knowledge to go. And as you learn, prepare to teach. "Connect" with *Connections*.

CHAPTER

The MacGyver Factor

Beads of perspiration begin to trickle down your face. The intense heat of the hostile, war-torn tropical Latin American country makes it almost impossible to breathe. The panic-stricken woman you just rescued from the roach-ridden guerrilla prison clings to your arm, just on the edge of hysteria. Your mission: to return her safely to her father, the ambassador. You have no weapons, no food, no transportation, and no way to communicate with the outside world. Surrounded by hostile enemy troops, you realize your barely adequate place of concealment will soon be discovered.

What do you do?

Frankly, I don't know what I would do. I don't know what you would do. But I do know what MacGyver would do. Star of the television adventure series by that name, MacGyver is the master of ingenuity. There doesn't seem to be any situation this miracle man can't handle. He's the enigma of modern crime drama, the man without weapons, the man with the **mind**. With his vast knowledge and creativity, he makes a reflective parabolic mirror from the remains of a blown-up jeep in the bushes where he is hiding. Focusing the sun's rays on some enemy ammunition, he creates an explosion and diversion to occupy the troops while he and the girl make their way to an abandoned farmer's shed. Finding bits and pieces of old materials and common household chemicals in the shed, he is able to create explosive devices for future protection. He gathers enough parts from a broken radio to create a homing device that signals the rescue helicopter to pick them up.

Fantastic? Yes. Obviously fictional. But how would you like to have a marketing manager like MacGyver?

The character of MacGyver personifies the tremendous freedom of the individual who operates from a knowledge of **principles**. He has great creative freedom because he knows so much and is able to apply that knowledge in a real variety of different circumstances. On the more serious side, the MacGyver Factor demonstrates what I call the **Principle of Principles**.

In the area of time management, as in most other areas in life, we are often bound by **practices**, specific ways of doing things. When we encounter situations for which a practice has not been prescribed, we often feel lost and incompetent.

But practices are mere facets of underlying **principles**. A person who understands principles can use or create a variety of implementing practices in different circumstances to accomplish his purpose.

So how do we recognize principles? To begin with, they are **timeless**. Throughout the ages, in a variety of circumstances, in different civilizations, in diverse literature, they have surfaced, like cream rising to the top. Unlike fads, principles are universal, they never go out of style, and they are recognized as fundamental to the vibrancy, the vitality and the longevity of a society or of an individual. INTEGRITY, for example, is an enduring principle without which civilizations have decayed and individuals have lost their ability to affect and influence their own lives as well as the lives of others.

Principles are also **self-validating**. Because we may have come in contact with them in one aspect of life, when we see them again, we may tend to pass them off as "common sense" and fail to appreciate their fundamental nature. For example, you may have experienced the "law of the harvest" as you worked in your garden. You discovered that you had to plant what you wanted to grow and nurture it if you expected to enjoy the results. But when it comes to setting your own personal goals, you may not have associated your success (or lack of it) to that same fundamental principle. Like Ali Hafed in Russell Conwell's *Acres of Diamonds*, instead of realizing the value of the timeless principle you already had within your grasp, you may have wasted time searching for answers in far less fruitful fields. The idea that principles are self-validating can give us greater confidence in what we already know.

In addition, principles are **empowering**. While practices are limited and restraining, principles generate freedom by broadening our knowledge base and increasing options and creativity. With the MacGyver Factor, you can still get four by adding two plus two—but you could also consider one plus three, ninety-two minus eighty-eight, two hundred twenty-eight divided by fifty-seven, an infinite variety of fractional combinations or the square root of sixteen. Principles also provide the power of constancy, and, as we will discuss later, they actually remove obstacles to growth and accomplishment.

So principles can be recognized because they are timeless, self-validating and empowering. In determining how to apply them, it is often helpful to use the following model:

1. **Purpose** (define the objective; what are you trying to accomplish?)

2. **Principles** (identify the principles that might apply)

3. **Strategy** (based on conditions, available resources and skill, determine what strategy would be most effective and efficient)

Resurrecting MacGyver for demonstration purposes, we might say he had his **purpose** clear in deciding to create a diversion. He knew the **principles** of physics which enabled him to see the resources around him. Various options undoubtedly went through his mind, but as he considered the conditions, available resources, and his own skill, the most effective **strategy** clicked into place. He focused the sun's rays on the ammunition store and caused it to explode.

The troops were diverted; MacGyver got the results he wanted. Had he been thinking in terms of practices, MacGyver and the ambassador's daughter might even now be sitting in that roach-ridden Latin American prison, berating the fact that they couldn't find a hand grenade.

Although we don't usually have to face hostile guerrillas and jungle heat, you and I do have a lot of forces working against us as we try to create clarity of direction and congruency of action in our lives. Using Lewin's Force Field Analysis model, we might visualize our situation as something like this:

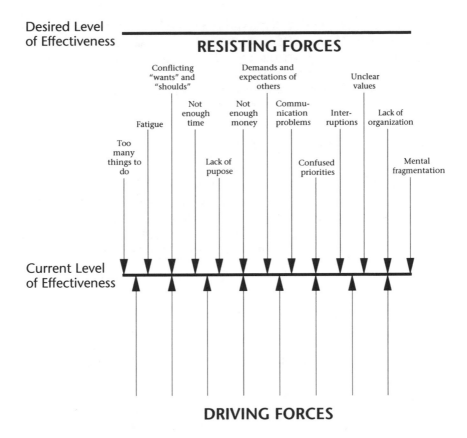

What, then, are the principles we can use to increase the driving forces and decrease the resisting forces, making change and growth possible? I have identified eight major high-leverage principles involved in significantly raising the level of personal effectiveness.

PRINCIPLE ONE: VISION

Vision is seeing **clearly**. It is being on top of the mountain and surveying the terrain instead of down in the valley hacking your way through the undergrowth.

Vision is seeing **contextually**. It is recognizing things as parts of other related things and being aware of connections.

Vision is seeing **imaginatively**. It is using the powers of the mind to look ahead at potential opportunities and impacts. It is mental creation that precedes physical realization.

Vision is seeing **alternatively**. It is awareness of options, choices and better ways.

PRINCIPLE TWO: IDENTITY

In attempting to put together the puzzle that defines who and what we are, many of us carry around some 5,000 pieces when all we really need is 500. Friends, relatives, merchants, politicians, and society in general all hand us pieces as we go along which describe what they think part of us should be.

But the fact is that **we** put the puzzle together. Though these pieces may be floating around in our thoughts, **we are greater than our thoughts**. We can think about them. And the sooner we realize what parts fit and throw away the ones that don't, the less confusion and incongruity we have to deal with in managing our time. We are free to act as individuals, knowing who we are as opposed to who others are and as opposed to the influences that would seek to shape us without our consent, and knowing who we are in harmony with our own deepest feelings and directions.

Identity also means **we are responsible** for ourselves and our choices. It means we do not blame other people or circumstances, but we accept personal responsibility for our lives and recognize our right to change.

PRINCIPLE THREE: PURPOSE

Purpose defines **destination, location, value** and **evaluation.** A clear purpose identifies where you want to go. It helps you analyze where you are in relation to where you want to go. It provides a standard against which you can measure the value of various potential activities and determine their relative worth. And it helps you evaluate the results of the things you do in terms of how effectively and efficiently they move you toward your destination.

Also, importantly, purpose and context give meaning and joy to daily activities that might otherwise seem mundane. If your purpose is to provide a comfortable and beautiful home for the people you love, mowing the lawn or carrying out the garbage doesn't seem all that bad.

PRINCIPLE FOUR: ORDER

Order is **system** and **arrangement**.

Order is also "first things first." It is **priorities** (some things are more important than others). It is **seasons** (some things are important now; some will be more important later). It is **deferred gratification** (some things need to be done now so that other things can be done later). It is **preparation** (some things need to be done ahead of other things). And it is **position** (some things, such as money, are servants and not masters).

PRINCIPLE FIVE: CONCENTRATION

Calling on MacGyver once again, we can clearly see the power of concentration. By focusing the rays of the sun, MacGyver was able to create a powerful force for accomplishing his purpose. The sunlight was there all the time, diffused in the atmosphere. But concentrating it on one particular point harnessed and directed the power to accomplish what it otherwise could not have done. Our diffused time and energies can be concentrated for powerful results.

PRINCIPLE SIX: INTEGRITY

Integrity is acting in accordance with your deepest values without compromise. We each have what I like to call a "personal integrity account" into which we are constantly making either deposits or withdrawals. When we set and achieve goals we deeply feel are right, when we keep commitments and promises to ourselves, when we act in harmony with our inner values in a **moment of truth**, we add to that account. When we justify exceptions to our own determinations, when we fail to meet a goal, when our actions fall short of our convictions, we make withdrawals. Whether our account is in the red or the black powerfully affects our confidence, our level of stress, our creativity, and our ability to relate meaningfully to others.

PRINCIPLE SEVEN: HARMONY

Of all the principles, harmony is one of the most intuitive. We cringe when we hear discordant music; we tense when there is discord in our lives.

Inner harmony is the selection, resolution and balance of a number of independent melodies. It is the selection of appropriate and realistic goals congruent with inner values. It is the resolution of wants and shoulds. It is the balance of work, family, community and personal priorities.

Inner harmony is also the prelude to harmonious relationships with others.

PRINCIPLE EIGHT: PROGRESSION

Nothing left to itself remains as it is; in other words, **the only time you can coast in life is when you're going downhill.**

To ignore growth, development and progress is not to remain static; it is to degenerate. If you don't exercise your body, for example, it does not remain in a constant state of health. Muscles grow flabby, plaque accumulates in the blood vessels and bones grow brittle with decreasing circulation. If you don't exercise your mind, your ability to learn decreases and you forget much of what you have already learned. You are either progressing or regressing, but you are never standing still.

These, then, are eight timeless, self-validating empowering principles of effective time management. Referring again to the Force Field Analysis model, it becomes easy to see how strengthening these principles in our lives not only has a powerful impact on the driving forces that give us upward thrust in our effort to live effectively, but also acts to dissipate a number of the forces of resistance that hold us back.

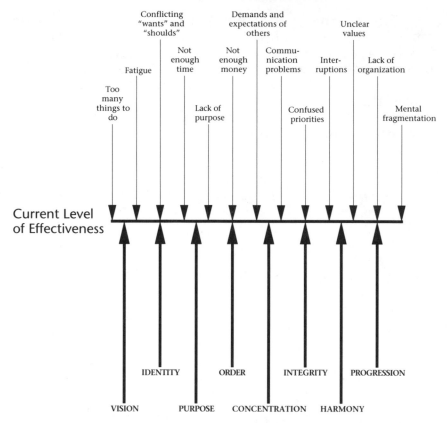

Following our model, we can identify our purpose as "connecting what we **want** to do, what we feel we **should** do, and what we actually **do** in order to manage our time more effectively."

Remember that effective strategies are based on conditions, available resources, and skill. This means that the most effective strategy to accomplish this purpose may be different for different individuals. The relative value of a particular strategy can be determined by a simple three-point test:

1. **Harmony**—Is it in harmony with timeless principles? (Seeking to close a business deal through dishonesty and deceit would not be a valuable strategy.) Is it in harmony with the conditions, my available resources and current skill level? (Solving the problem of office space by constructing new offices when there is no money in the budget would not be a harmonious strategy.)

2. **Effectiveness**—Does it bring the desired results?

3. **Efficiency**—Does the outcome justify the input? Is there a better way?

The strategies suggested in this book have been carefully selected because they have brought tremendous results in hundreds of lives. I strongly suggest that you try them, experience the results and get a feeling for the implementation of the principles. Then, if you determine another strategy will bring you the same or better results more efficiently, go with what works best for you. The MacGyver Factor gives you the personal freedom to do that.

CHAPTER

The VIP Connection

I didn't pay too much attention as my wife answered the phone. With three teenagers in the house, she does that a lot. But when I heard her incredulous response and saw her face, I knew that this was nothing ordinary. She turned to me almost in disbelief and said, "John is dead! He was killed in an auto accident last night!"

John was a close friend of the family, a frequent visitor in our home. He had a lovely wife and six children at home. And all of a sudden, he was gone.

It doesn't take more than one experience like that to get you thinking pretty deeply about your own life. Suddenly the things that occupy your mind every day seem a little trivial compared to the bigger questions, the deeper issues, the fundamental essence of who and what you are and why you're here.

It's not always the death of someone close that opens the door to a perspective expanding experience. I've had the same kinds of feelings traveling in an airplane with an engine threatening to fail. I've had them stretched out in a sleeping bag in the Uinta Mountains looking up into a sky filled with a thousand stars. I've had them walking through the dusty roads of Cochebamba, driving by my old high school after 24 years, holding my wife's hand as she gave birth to our child.

It is during those times of deeper searching, of expanded perspective, that we begin to establish what I call the "VIP CONNECTION." The "VIP" stands for the principles involved—VISION, IDENTITY and PURPOSE. I also call it "VIP" because I believe that you and I and everyone else in this world truly are "Very Important Persons," each with unique talents and great contributions to make. VIP is that inner connection that hooks us up to our own deepest values and possibilities.

As we come in touch with our own potential and begin to deeply harmonize our inner imperatives, all the peripheral wants and shoulds that constantly float in and out of our mental awareness seem to either coalesce into a unified sense of personal mission or burst and disappear. A lot of what we think we "want" to do is really what advertising wizards have conditioned us to want to do. Or maybe it's something we really do want to do, but, as we look more deeply, we find it's not nearly as important as other, more lasting things. Much of what we feel we "should" do we find to be a reflection of what someone else thinks we should do, or perhaps it is excess baggage we have carried with us for years which has no foundation in our own personal set of values now. It is during these times of VIP connection that we are able to discard many of the puzzle pieces that have been handed to us by others and determine for ourselves what pieces fit the picture that belongs to us.

These are sobering times, meaningful times, often great times. When you really come to grips with your inner self, you feel like singing, "On a Clear Day You Can See Forever." You feel as if you're on the top of a mountain and the things you deal with every day are somehow smaller, more in perspective. You can see where you're going. Maybe you can even see the path to get you there.

But the vision doesn't last forever. You get caught back up in the routine of daily living and find it slipping farther and farther away from your conscious awareness. And before long, if you don't have some way to keep it before you or if another perspective expanding experience doesn't come along, the connection is broken and the vision becomes almost totally obscured.

The challenge, then, of keeping that connection strong becomes the challenge of capturing the vision and keeping it before us on a regular basis. I believe the single most effective strategy to accomplish this purpose is a **written creed** or **personal mission statement**.

A mission statement contains three basic elements. The first is what you want to **be**—what character strengths you want to have, what qualities you want to develop. The second is what you want to **do**—what you want to accomplish, what contributions you want to make. And the third is the **values** and **principles** upon which your being and doing are based.

Interestingly, statements of this kind have been discovered in the records of various civilizations throughout the ages. Modern history provides us with a number of such statements written by individuals or organizations we easily recognize for their outstanding accomplishment and contribution.

I think the strength of the personal mission statement is fourfold. First, it forces you to think deeply about your life. It causes you to expand your perspective, to examine your innermost thoughts and feelings, to resolve the conflicts between wants and shoulds on a very essential level, and to identify the purpose of your life and what is really important to you. Second, writing it down forces you to clarify and express succinctly your deepest values and aspirations. Third, writing the statement imprints your values and purposes firmly in your mind so that it becomes a part of you instead of something you just thought about once. And finally, it gives you a tangible tool to keep that vision of your self constantly before you.

Writing a personal mission statement involves three steps.

STEP ONE: PROACTIVELY EXPAND YOUR PERSPECTIVE

Because unplanned perspective expanding experiences are, by their very nature, unpredictable events, you can take a proactive approach, move into Quadrant II and plan your own.

The end result of these experiences would be a written personal mission statement, reflecting what you want to be and do in life and the values and principles that will empower you.

There are a number of exercises that have proven successful in expanding perspective. Some of them can be done rather quickly with good, but limited, results. These would include such mental gymnastics as the following:

1. Plan your own funeral. Sit down in a quiet place where you can relax and let your imagination carry you to your last recognition in life. Visualize your body resting peacefully as friends and loved ones gather to honor you. Imagine who would speak at the service. What would they say? What qualities of character would you be remembered for? What outstanding contributions would they mention? As they review the major events of your life, do you feel pleased and satisfied? Look around at the people there. Do you feel you have made an important difference in their lives?

2. Try to imagine how you would feel if you were suddenly told you had only six months to live. What are the things you would want to do in those six months? Take a few moments and write them down.

For a less visual, more logical experience, you could use Lewin's Force Field Analysis model to identify where you want to be, where you are now, and the factors that are working for and against your effort to change.

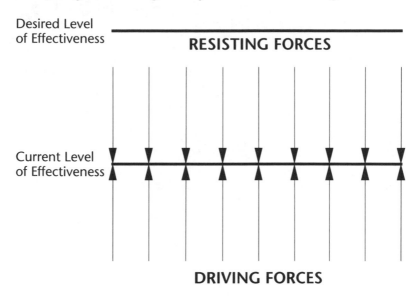

You could answer questions such as:

- What is the ideal situation? How would I spend my time? What would be the results?
- What is my current situation? How do I spend my time now?
- What are the specific factors that keep me from the ideal? What can I do to weaken or remove them?
- What are the specific factors that move me toward the ideal? What can I do to strengthen or add to them?

Other exercises that require a greater investment of time but generally bring more meaningful results might include a more in-depth experience like one my wife had recently. She has kept a personal journal on a fairly consistent basis for a number of years, which, in itself, is a powerful connecting activity. At this particular time in her life, she felt a need to reevaluate and realign her priorities. So I arranged to manage home and family needs for a couple of days and she went alone to an inn, where she spent hours reviewing the pages she had written. As she viewed her life from a more removed perspective, she was able to identify repeating patterns which could not be seen from day to day. In the overview, she found the personal direction she needed and returned home refreshed and much more connected to her deepest values.

Another very effective experience can be created by a planned retreat in a wilderness setting. There seems to be a harmony and balance in nature that reminds us of the principles of timelessness, of forces beyond the sometimes petty challenges of our own lives. The dramatic difference in environment for those of us who live and work in confined spaces creates an awareness that we are greater than our habits and/or environment. We can listen to our thoughts and think about our thoughts. We can stand apart from our habits and look at ourselves in a way that enables us to take charge and to plan the kind of change we want to effect.

I suggest one of the best ways to begin to find your VIP connection is to take this book, some paper and a pencil with you to a favorite place where you can be alone. It may be the seashore, it may be up in the mountains, it may be in an easy chair by the fire. But isolate yourself from phones, neighbors, friends, and even family. Plan to spend several hours by yourself. Clear your mind and try to really open up to your innermost feelings.

Take your time and thoughtfully answer questions such as the ones below. If you use these questions, I suggest you overview them first. Some people prefer to begin with the more specific questions listed first and then move into a general feeling about their missions in life. Others prefer to start with the more general questions, such as 13, 14 and 15, and to gradually get more specific.

Some people prefer to read over these questions for a feeling of the level of thinking needed to write a personal mission statement, and then simply let their thoughts interact for several days or even weeks. Sometimes, the resulting mission statement emerges in a relatively short time as it all seems to "come together."

While some have to labor deeply to shift perspective, sort out values and express thoughts and feelings, others write quickly after an extensive period of thinking time. The "best" way to do it is whatever works for you.

1. When I think of the one person who has made the strongest positive impact on my life, I believe he (or she) has had a powerful influence on me because:

    _____
    _____
    _____
    _____

2. The qualities of character I most admire in others are:

    _____
    _____
    _____
    _____
    _____

3. I am impressed by the following attitudes:

    _____
    _____
    _____
    _____

4. The three people who seem to me to have accomplished the most in their lives are:

    _____
    _____
    _____

Some of the things they accomplished are:

_____

_____

_____

_____

5. The people I know who seem to be the happiest are:

_____

_____

I think they are happy because:

_____

_____

_____

6. If my resources were such that I did not have to work for a living or I could do anything I wanted, I would:

_____

_____

_____

_____

_____

_____

The reason I would do that is:

_____

_____

I think I would do it for (how long?):

_____

_____

7. When I don't have to do something, what I like to do most is:

_____
_____
_____
_____
_____
_____

8. The moments of greatest happiness and satisfaction come to me when:

_____
_____
_____
_____
_____

9. People who know me well think I'm very good at:

_____
_____
_____
_____
_____

10. When I daydream, I sometimes see myself doing something great like:

_____
_____
_____
_____
_____

11. When all things are considered, what I really do best is:

_____

_____

_____

_____

_____

12. At this point in my life, the most admirable thing about me is:

_____

_____

_____

_____

_____

13. The three or four most important things to me are:

_____

_____

_____

_____

_____

14. When I look at my **work** life in perspective, these are the activities that are of the most worth:

_____

_____

_____

_____

_____

_____

If I were to categorize these high value activities into three or four groups, I would use the following categories:

_____

_____

_____

_____

_____

15. When I look at my **personal** life in perspective, these are the activities that are of most worth:

_____

_____

_____

_____

_____

_____

If I were to categorize these high value activities into three or four groups, I would use the following categories:

_____

_____

_____

_____

16. The things I do (or that I could do) best that would be of most worth to others are:

_____

_____

_____

_____

17. The talents I feel I have that no one else really knows about are:

_____

_____

_____

18. Though I may have dismissed the thought many times before for various reasons, at times I have felt that what I should really do is:

_____

_____

_____

_____

19. If I really did some of the things I feel I should do, I would:

_____

_____

_____

_____

_____

20. When I review questions 6-8, I can think of something that I could do that would harmonize those feelings with my answers to questions 18 and 19. That is:

_____

_____

_____

_____

_____

_____

After thinking about it, some of the elements I would like to have in my mission statement are:

What I'd like to be: **What I'd like to do:**

_____   _____
_____   _____
_____   _____
_____   _____
_____   _____
_____   _____

The values and principles I choose for my foundation:

_____   _____
_____   _____
_____   _____
_____   _____
_____   _____
_____   _____

One other type of exercise that gives added dimension is to look at life over a period of time. In a day of increasing life expectancy, there can be several seasons to life. Retirement now brings with it a realistic expectation of 20 years or more, opening the door to the possibility of a second career that can add great meaning to life. Often the second career is more of a choice than the first. Experience, resources and opportunity open many doors that were previously closed.

The following exercise is an excellent one to go through with your spouse if you're married. You may be thinking of a second career as a patron of the arts living in a downtown condominium, while he may be planning to purchase a horse ranch in Montana.

Having a sense of purpose often will improve the quality of life now as well as in the future. The vision of later years can revive enthusiasm for your purposes now as you realize these are not the only purposes you may accomplish. In the first column on the following chart, list the things you would really like to do at some time in your life. Then shade in the boxes, indicating when you might do each of these things. Five to ten year increments are exact enough for the purpose of this exercise.

Things I want to do	When (Approximate Age)								
	20	30	40	50	60	70	80	90	100

For added perspective, go back now and note the year you will be each age. For example, if you are now 30, figure out what year you will be 40, 50, 60 and so on, and write the date above the corresponding age.

As you can see, there is no one "right way" to expand your perspective. With the MacGyver mentality, you can accomplish your purpose with any principle-based strategy that works for you.

One pitfall you want to be certain to avoid in expanding your self-awareness is misinterpreting what you may feel is a personal weakness as a primary direction in life. Some years ago, I worked with the personnel department of a large corporation. On my staff was Fred, a man who conducted employment interviews with about average performance.

I had the occasion to ask him one day if he would do one of the tasks I delegated to staff members on a rotating basis. It was a project which required statistical analysis of a number of factors in the department. Fred agreed, but when he turned in the assignment, I was astounded. I had never seen the quality of work he produced on a report like this. I immediately went to find him.

"Fred!" I exclaimed. "This is phenomenal! I've never seen anything done so well."

Fred gave me a little smile. " I enjoyed doing it," he replied. "I've always been good in math."

Now he had me puzzled. "Could I ask you a question?" I ventured.

"Sure," he replied.

"Why in the world are you in recruiting and employment? You seem to be doing all right, but you obviously have a great talent in the area of analysis. Why did you choose this particular job?"

Fred looked a little sheepish. "That's just it," he replied. "I know I'm strong in analysis. But I never have been good with people. I felt I needed to improve in that area of my life."

I shared with Fred an important concept of effectiveness I have seen validated time and time again. By focusing on our strengths, we not only increase our productivity and personal happiness, but we also use our unique talents to make significant contributions that would otherwise not be made. Of course we need to improve in areas of weakness. But to become overly focused on weakness keeps us from connecting to our inner strength and areas of greatest contribution.

A short time later, when an opening for an analytical job came up in another department, with Fred's approval, I recommended him for the job. He thoroughly enjoyed the assignment and performed with excellence. Within a year, he was managing the section. Interestingly, as his confidence grew in his new job, he became more relaxed about interacting with people and, for the most part, his weakness took care of itself.

In any perspective expanding experience, keep in mind that you will ultimately be seeking to give expression to the values and purposes that will create your inner guidance system. Remember to build on your strengths. Use the great talents and abilities you have. And also remember that **you can never build a life greater than its most noble purpose.** Those purposes that are outside self, higher than self, will empower and lift you to fulfill whatever tremendous potential you have as a "VIP."

STEP TWO: WRITE A PERSONAL MISSION STATEMENT

When you feel you have a fairly accurate idea of what you want to be and to do, try writing a rough draft of a personal mission statement. I would suggest that you carry the rough draft with you and make notes, additions and deletions for at least a month before you attempt another draft. It will probably take several re-writes before you feel satisfied with the result.*

When you do have a permanent copy, review it frequently. I strongly recommend that you commit it to memory. This will increase the power of the process to help you keep your vision clear and your values clearly in mind.

STEP THREE: EVALUATE

It's a good idea as you complete each draft of your personal mission statement to evaluate it carefully. In addition, as you change and grow, your perspectives and

---

* If you would like to receive some examples of mission statements—at no cost to you—please call 1-800-255-0777.

56

values may undergo some metamorphosis. It is important that you do not let your statement become outdated. Periodic review and evaluation can help you keep in touch with your own development and keep your statement in harmony with your deepest self.

Some questions that may be helpful as you evaluate your mission statement are:

1. Is my mission based on my growing awareness of timeless proven principles? Which ones?

_____

_____

_____

_____

_____

_____

2. Do I feel this represents the best within me? What changes could I make to improve it?

_____

_____

_____

_____

_____

_____

3. During my best moments, how do I feel about what this represents?

_____

_____

_____

_____

_____

_____

4. Do I feel direction, purpose, challenge and some motivation when I review this statement? In what ways?

    _____

    _____

    _____

    _____

    _____

5. What strategies and skills will help me accomplish what I have written?

    _____

    _____

    _____

    _____

    _____

6. What do I need to start doing now to be where I want to be tomorrow?

    _____

    _____

    _____

    _____

    _____

    _____

    _____

I think it's hard to overemphasize the value of the VIP CONNECTION. I've seen a lot of people working to be more efficient at what they do, but grossly unhappy because they are doing the wrong things. Let me tell you about the tremendous difference the VIP CONNECTION made to Tom.

I met Tom at a seminar for university students. When I asked him to introduce himself and tell a little about his goals, he indicated that he was majoring in civil engineering. Later during the seminar, he was given the opportunity to share with others what he would do if he had a month with no demands on his time and unlimited funds.

"That's easy!" Tom replied enthusiastically. "I'd buy a table saw, a planer, and...oh, lots of other tools. I'd set them up in my garage, get all the kids in the neighborhood together, and we'd build things—tables, playhouses, furniture. It would be great!"

As I noticed the shining eyes, I couldn't help but remember the apathy with which he had announced his college major a few moments before.

"You really like to teach, don't you?" I asked.

"I love it!" he said simply.

"And you enjoy working with tools?"

"Oh, you bet!"

"How are you enjoying your classes in civil engineering?"

"Oh, I don't know. There's good money in engineering..." His voice dropped off.

"Did it ever occur to you that they **pay** people to teach kids how to build things with tools?"

As an important link in Tom's VIP CONNECTION suddenly fell into place and he realized that he could do what he really wanted to do in life and get paid for it, his expression was incredulous. His wants and shoulds converged on a much deeper level and he suddenly realized that his avocation could be his vocation. That one connection saved Tom years of the frustration and inner conflict many people live with every day.

The VIP CONNECTION is the first and most fundamental link of effective time management. It is ridiculous to consider saving minutes when you may be wasting years. There is no planner, no calendar, no speed-reading course or time-motion study that can save you that kind of time.

If you live to be 80 years old, you will have spent almost 27 years of that time sleeping and another 3 1/2 years eating. You can't afford to waste the remaining 49 1/2 years doing what you really don't want to do. After all you're a "VIP!"

CHAPTER

The Translation Connection

Almost every time I address a group on the subject of effective time management, I have at least one person in the audience who has had a powerful perspective-expanding experience fairly recently. I occasionally have some who have even committed their realizations to writing. But I find they are usually deeply frustrated because it hasn't really made a difference in what they do each day. They are still living in Quadrants I and III, mostly responding to the apparently urgent instead of doing the important. These people are, in fact, even more frustrated than most because they have a greater awareness of what they deeply feel they need to do in their lives. Somehow, the vision never gets **translated** into daily activity.

I remember having the same feeling once when I walked into my garage after a family camping trip. There were sleeping bags, mess kits, back packs, space blankets, tents, tarps, canteens and various other camping necessities all dumped right there on the floor. It was all great stuff and it was there in the garage where it was supposed to be. But **WHAT DO YOU DO WITH IT?**

Thanks to that timeless, empowering principle of ORDER, I was able to bring some semblance of meaning to the melee in my garage. I cleared some shelves and labelled them, putting the sleeping bags in one place, the back packs in another. After a while, things looked a lot better, and I thought there was the minute possibility I might even consider another camping trip someday.

Having the big picture in mind does not automatically empower us to do something meaningful with it. There's too much there to handle all at once; it's simply too big to fit, *en masse*, into any given moment of time. And that's where ORDER comes in. And PURPOSE. And HARMONY. And a wonderful strategy called **roles and goals.**

We live our lives in terms of roles, not in the sense of role playing, but in the sense of authentic parts we've chosen to fill. We have roles at work, in the family, in the community, and in other areas of life. These roles become a natural framework to give ORDER to what we want to be and to do.

One way of looking at it is to consider the way the postmaster sorts the mail. He puts it into various slots according to its destination. If we picture the slots as the roles in our lives, we put different amounts of time and energy into various roles every day.

Take some time and try to identify the various roles in your life. **Roles must, of course, be in harmony with and grow out of your personal mission statement.** There is no set way to define your roles. Another person doing almost the same things you do might well define the roles differently. The important thing is that you feel comfortable with the roles you define.

You may want to define your family role as simply "family member." Or, you may choose to divide it into two roles, "husband" and "father," or "wife" and "mother." Some areas of your life, such as your job, may involve several roles. For example, you may have a role in administration, one in marketing, one in personnel and one in long-range planning. Research has shown that it is ineffective to attempt to mentally manage more than seven categories, so you should never have more than a total of seven roles. Sometimes this requires combining functions, such as administration/finance, or personnel/team-building. You may also want to have one role that reflects personal development.

A product development executive might define his roles like this:

1. Individual/Personal Development
2. Husband/Father
3. Manager-New Products
4. Manager-Research
5. Manager-Staff Development
6. Manager-Administration
7. United Way Chairman

A part-time real estate salesperson might list the following roles:

1. Mother
2. Home Manager
3. Salesperson-Prospects
4. Salesperson-Financing/Administration
5. Salesperson-Properties
6. PTA Vice President
7. Individual-Hobbies/Development

Now try your hand at giving expression to the various roles in your life. You may have to work with them a while before they feel right to you.

Roles

1. _____

2. _____

3. _____

4. _____

5. _____

6. _____

7. _____

One of the greatest results of defining your roles is that it increases your ability to create HARMONY, or balance between the different facets of your life. With the increased perspective of overview, you will be less likely to find yourself succeeding in one area at the expense of other, possibly even more important, areas.

After you've completed the first part of the roles and goals strategy, you are ready to apply the principle of CONCENTRATION or focus. Look back at your first role and identify the one, two or three most important things you could do in that role during the next year that would be based on principles and congruent with the values expressed in your mission statement. These become your **yearly goals**. Our product development executive might have written:

1. Individual/Personal Development

    -   Implement a regular program of physical exercise

    -   Devote at least one week during the year to a concentrated development activity, such as a seminar

    -   Develop a personal mission statement

Our part-time real estate salesperson might list:

1. Mother

    -   Build my relationship with John by becoming more involved in his areas of personal interest (attend basketball games, etc.)

    -   Develop the habit of empathic listening

    -   Enjoy motherhood more on a daily basis

Because you may not be quite ready to commit to a specific action in a particular area, you may find it beneficial to think of your goals in terms of **determinations** and **concentrations**. **Determinations** would be specific things that, no matter what, you are determined to do, such as daily exercise. When you set a determination, you put your integrity on the line. **Concentrations**, on the other hand, would be areas of pursuit you focus your efforts around, such as "enjoy motherhood more on a daily basis" from the example above. Concentrations are not goals in the traditional sense of the word. They are not measurable, time-bound specific actions; they are, instead, areas of heightened awareness in which you want to create a focus. Concentrations can have value because they enable you to channel your interest without risking your integrity when you are not quite ready to commit to specific action.

Now go ahead and list up to three most important goals for each role you have defined.

Roles   Goals

1. _____   _____
                           _____

2. _____   _____
                           _____
                           _____

3. _____   _____
                           _____
                           _____

4. _____   _____
                           _____
                           _____

5. _____   _____
                           _____
                           _____

6. _____   _____
                           _____
                           _____

7. _____   _____
                           _____
                           _____
                           _____

Now take a look at what you have just written. You have just put ORDER in your life. You have also created HARMONY in balancing the various roles you have chosen to fulfill.

In addition, you have applied the principle of CONCENTRATION by identifying the most important things you can do during the coming months in every area of your life. You are now ready to use the Weekly Worksheet to translate those important activities into a workable action plan.

The critical link between mission and daily action is forged in the second major strategy of this chapter: **Quadrant II weekly organizing**. This is the blueprint, the mental creation, the **moment of clarity** where your roles and goals become the primary influencing factors as you plan the activities you will do each day. Rather than simply planning out the week based on what happens to be in front of you, you are proactively determining which hours during the week will be invested in the things that you have decided are most important. It is here that the foundation is laid for reversing the tendency to respond to the apparently urgent, creating the opportunity to do the truly important.

There are principles which seem to reinforce the idea of organizing on a weekly basis. But at this point, it is sufficient to say that the strategy is extremely effective because the week is a complete little patch out of the fabric of life. It has the weekend, it has the evening, it has the workday. It is close enough to the activities of the day that it becomes highly relevant, but far enough away to provide context and perspective. It also enables us to see that roles that may not seem balanced in a 24 hour period can be balanced in the longer-term perspective of the week.

Before reading farther, take a careful look at the Weekly Worksheet on page 79. As we go through the planning process you may want to refer to it from time to time.

The first step in Quadrant II organizing is to set aside a specific time in a quiet place each week to preview your week. Then take out your Weekly Worksheet and again write down your roles.

Roles/Goals

Key Roles	This Week's Goals
1 *Individual-Personal Development*	
2 *Husband/Father*	
3 *Manager— New Products*	
4 *Manager— Research*	
5 *Manager— Staff Development*	
6 *Manager— Administration*	
7 *United Way Chairman*	

The process of writing down your roles brings back to memory almost immediately some of the feelings and phrases of your mission statement and begins to build up the context in which you want to plan your time. Your roles will tend to change somewhat over time, but in most cases will not change weekly. Investing these few seconds in writing them down is very important.

The next step, then, is to review your goals in each role and to ask yourself, "**This week**, what are the one, two or three most important things I can do to move forward in that role and to accomplish the goals I'm trying to achieve?" Write them down on your Weekly Worksheet.

Roles/Goals

Key Roles	This Week's Goals
1 Individual-Personal Development	Rough draft of mission statement Register for seminar Visit Frank in hospital
2 Husband/Father	Home mgt./Karla's class Tim's science project Sarah's bike
3 Manager— New Products	Test market parameters Interview assistant candidates Study consumer survey
4 Manager— Research	Study last test results Work on bonding problem Network with Ken and Peter
5 Manager— Staff Development	Performance review with Janie Visit with Samuels
6 Manager— Administration	End of month reports Salary review report
7 United Way Chairman	Prepare agenda P.R. visit with Conklin Start next year's plan

You will probably be aware of a number of things you could do in each role, but remember to apply the maxim, **"you can do anything you want, but not everything."** Force yourself to prioritize and limit yourself to three.

Once that part of the organizing process is complete, begin to transfer your goals to specific times during the week. You will notice on the Weekly Worksheet that there are two kinds of areas for each day. One provides space to list priorities for the day; the other is divided into the hours for specific appointments. To build each important activity you have listed into your plan, either write it as a priority you are going to fit in on that particular day, or, more effectively, set an appointment with yourself to work on a particular goal at a specific time of the day. The box in the lower left-hand corner entitled "Sharpen the Saw" provides a place to plan vital renewing Quadrant II activities in each of four human dimensions that will be discussed in Chapter Nine.

Weekly Worksheet
Sample

The Weekly Worksheet		WEEK OF:	SUNDAY	MONDAY
Roles	**Goals**	**Weekly Priorities**	**Today's Priorities**	**Today's Priorities**
				Salary review
Individual–Pers. Development	Rough draft mission stmnt / Register seminar / Visit Frank in hospital			*Report*
Husband/ Father	Home mgt./Karla's class / Tim's science project / Sarah's bike			
Manager— New Products	Test market parameters / Interview ass't candidates / Study consumer survey		**Appointments/Commitments**	
			8 *Private time*	8
			Mission stmnt	
			9	9
Manager— Research	Study last test result / Work on bonding problem / Network with Ken & Peter			
			10	10
			11	11 *Assistant job*
Manager— Staff dvlpmnt	Performace review with Jamie / Visit with Samuels			*interviews*
			12	12
Manager— Administration	End of month reports / Salary review report		1	1
			2	2
United Way Chairman	Prepare agenda / P.R. visit with Conklin / Start next year's plan		3	3 *Frank–hospital*
			4	4
Sharpen the Saw			5	5
Physical			6	6
Mental			Evening	Evening
Spiritual				*Sarah's bike*
Social/Emotional				

TUESDAY	WEDNESDAY	THURSDAY	FRIDAY	SATURDAY
Today's Priorities	Today's Priorities	Today's Priorities	Today's Priorities	Today's Priorities
Send in seminar registration			Visit Samuels	

TUESDAY	WEDNESDAY	THURSDAY	FRIDAY	SATURDAY
8	8	8	8	8
9	9 Test market parameters	9 Bonding problem	9 Study test results	9
10	10	10	10	10
11	11	11	11	11
12	12	12 Performance	12 Conklin	12
1 Study consumer survey	1	1 review—Janie	1	1
2	2	2	2	2
3	3	3	3 EOM report	3
4	4	4	4	4
5	5	5 United Way agenda	5	5
6 Tim's project	6	6 Next years plans	6	6
Evening	Evening	Evening	Evening	Evening

Now, an appointment with yourself should be managed just like an appointment with anybody else. If you treat other people with value when they set an appointment, treat yourself with value.

Sometimes, appointments have to be changed. But treat yourself with the same courtesy and consideration as you would anyone else.

After you have scheduled time for the truly important, then review your calendar for other appointments and commitments you may have previously made. Evaluate these in the context of your goals, transferring those you decide to keep to your schedule and making plans to cancel or reschedule others. Then look at other valuable activities you may want to fit into the week. List them as Weekly Priorities to be transferred to the appropriate day and time as you can fit them in. This can be done either as you organize the week or as you later plan each day.

The Weekly Priorities area of your worksheet can also be used to list the telephone numbers of people you will be contacting or other information pertinent to the activities of the week.

Let me review those weekly organizing steps once more, as they are essential to completing the TRANSLATION CONNECTION.

1. Review and write down the roles you have selected based on your personal mission statement.

2. Look at your long-term goals in each role and ask yourself, "What are the one, two or three key things I need to do in that role this week?" Write those things down beside the role.

3. Transfer each key activity onto a specific day of the week, either in the list of priorities for the day, or, more favorably, as an appointment with yourself.

4. Review and evaluate previously-made appointments and consider other activities you may want to plan into your week.

5. Transfer appointments you decide to keep from your calendar to the appropriate day and time, make plans to cancel or reschedule others, and note other valuable activities you want to fit into the week as Weekly Priorities.

Now use the Weekly Worksheet found on page 79 and plan the next week of your life. As you do so, take a look at how many of the goals you naturally select are Quadrant II activities, such as building relationships, clarifying values, preventing crises, planning, preparing and re-creating. Organizing your week in the context of your deepest values as reflected in your personal mission statement, your chosen roles and your yearly goals transfers you almost automatically into Quadrant II. That is why **weekly organizing is the key to the TRANSLATION CONNECTION**.

Without weekly organizing, we tend to spend our days responding to the flood of Quadrant I and III activities that constantly clamor for our attention, trying (often without success) to "fit in" those important Quadrant II activities we **want** to do, we know we really **need** to do.

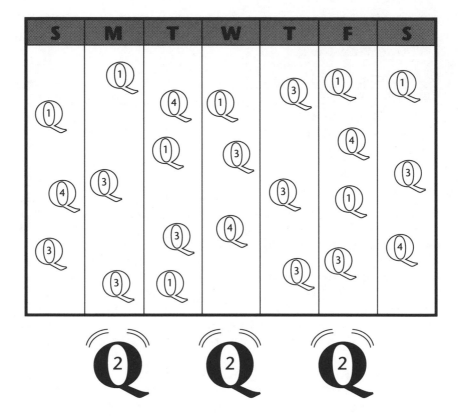

By organizing the week in the context of those important Quadrant II activities, we reverse that tendency. We create a framework to accomplish what is truly important, around which we can then "fit in" the sometimes less meaningful activities of other quadrants.

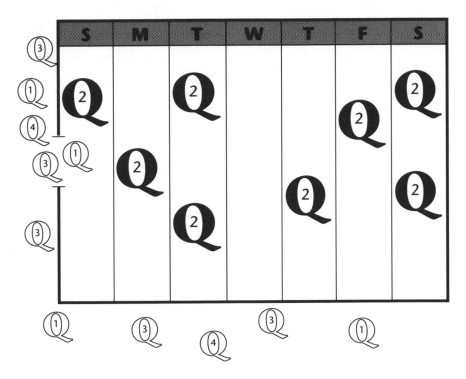

As you organize your week, ask yourself this question: "If I went forward this next seven days and did even half of those Quadrant II things which I've just written down, and I did that every week for the next year, what would happen to the quality of my life and all the roles I see for myself? What if I did them all?"

This is putting ORDER, HARMONY, and CONCENTRATION into your life. This is translating what is really important to you into a workable plan for action on a weekly basis. This is the TRANSLATION CONNECTION.

Weekly Worksheet

The Weekly Worksheet		WEEK OF:	SUNDAY	MONDAY
Roles	Goals	Weekly Priorities	Today's Priorities	Today's Priorities
			Appointments/Commitments	
			8	8
			9	9
			10	10
			11	11
			12	12
			1	1
			2	2
			3	3
			4	4
			5	5
			6	6
			Evening	Evening

Sharpen the Saw

Physical

Mental

Spiritual

Social/Emotional

TUESDAY	WEDNESDAY	THURSDAY	FRIDAY	SATURDAY
Today's Priorities	Today's Priorities	Today's Priorities	Today's Priorities	Today's Priorities

Appointments/Commitments			Appointments/Commitments	
8	8	8	8	8
9	9	9	9	9
10	10	10	10	10
11	11	11	11	11
12	12	12	12	12
1	1	1	1	1
2	2	2	2	2
3	3	3	3	3
4	4	4	4	4
5	5	5	5	5
6	6	6	6	6
Evening	Evening	Evening	Evening	Evening

SPECIAL SECTION

Timely Tips From Quadrant II

*This is a special section devoted to the proposition that all men (or women) are **not** created equal in their ability to effectively organize a week. These "timely tips" may come in handy when you sit down to organize the next seven days of your life.*

1. PLAN TIME TO PREPARE

Many activities become urgent as a result of lack of proper preparation. One of the quickest ways to move into Quadrant II is to scan ahead during weekly organizing and determine what needs to happen when, and what you need to do to get ready for it. Then plan time to prepare.

*For example, if you have a meeting on Friday morning at which you are supposed to make a presentation, you may need to set aside some time on Wednesday to concentrate and prepare. If you plan to work in your garden on Saturday, you may need to arrange to go to the store on Thursday night and purchase seeds or tools. The successful experiences most of us would like to have in life are rarely an accident; they are almost always an achievement, the result of careful planning and thorough preparation. The **moment of clarity** when we organize the week gives us the perspective to set aside the time necessary to make that preparation possible.*

2. GIVE YOURSELF TIME ESTIMATE FEEDBACK

Some people seem to be able to accurately estimate the amount of time it will take them to complete a project or perform a task. And then there's the rest of the human race.

For most of us, learning to estimate accurately takes a bit of work. We plan to do a project during the morning and wind up spending all day on it and even working overtime. To improve our time estimate accuracy is to greatly impact our ability to plan and achieve.

Learning how to do that is a lot like playing golf. You know where you want the ball to go, but sometimes you hit it short and sometimes you hit it long. As you watch where your balls land, you learn to estimate how far you can hit the ball with a particular club. And as you practice, you learn which club to select and how to hit the ball the desired distance more and more often.

An effective way to improve your ability to accurately estimate the time you need to complete a particular task is to give yourself some feedback. As you organize your week, jot down beside your activities how much time you think it will take to complete them. When you do them, jot down the time it actually took.

Over a period of time, you will become more accurate. Practice makes perfect—that's par for the course.

3. USE TIME ZONES

Time zones are large, interchangeable blocks of time set aside for specific important activities. For example, perhaps family activity is a high value with you and you usually reserve Saturday mornings for family type activities. You might want to block out that time as you organize your week. This is not an appointment or a commitment that you have made in the sense that every Saturday morning, without fail, that is exactly what you will do. The fluidity of circumstances in most people's lives would make that impractical. But as you plan other activities and goals, you *will have the tendency to keep that time reserved and to focus family activities to some degree toward that time.*

Perhaps you are active in a local community project or a service club that has meetings on Thursday evenings two or three weeks out of the month. To block out Thursday evening as a time for your service club could be a very useful thing to do. And on the weeks when no meeting is held, you could use the time for preparation, working on the membership roster, or whatever else you may need to do. This gives you an excellent opportunity to invest in Quadrant II activities in that role.

In your job, you may want to block out one morning a week for one-on-one staff interviews. When people want to see you, you can channel your appointments toward that established time zone. You might set aside another block of time during the week to prospect for new clients, read trade journals, or work on long-term planning.

The idea is not to fill the entire week with time zones, but to set aside a few specific time periods to provide focus for high priority activities and during which you can group similar activities.

There are a number of advantages in using time zones. To begin with, of course, you have the time blocked out for high priority, often Quadrant II, activities. It also gives a sense of order to your life that other people become aware of and respond to. If they know you set aside Thursday nights for club work, rather than interrupting you throughout the week, they know they can probably reach you on club matters then and you will be available and focused.

The fact that time zones are generally interchangeable allows for flexibility in the schedule without sacrificing allocated time in the overall week. For example, if some friends suddenly found they could not attend a concert on a Thursday night when you didn't have a meeting and they offered you tickets for your family, you could switch your family time zone to Thursday, do your club work Saturday morning, and still have done what was most important in the course of the week.

Time zones, in effect, provide an orderly overlay for the week.

4. KEEP "PERHAPS" LISTS

You constantly come in contact with ideas and insights which give birth to thoughts of things you could do with your time. You may read a book or attend a seminar or take part in a meeting or talk with an associate, and you come away from the experience saying, "Oh, I really ought to do that." You want to keep track of that idea, but you're not ready to incorporate it as a goal.

If you're like most people, you probably let these ideas wander around in an over-cluttered cerebral waiting room, floating in and out of awareness, distracting you from the task at hand and causing a vague uneasiness of something not yet done. Or maybe you write them down on a generic "to do" list that seems to collect items faster than they can ever be accomplished, mingles top priority items with things that don't really matter much, and constantly reminds you of all you haven't done. The resulting confusion of priorities and negative reinforcement do not appear to me to be very effective in keeping focused and energized.

Far more effective, I believe, is the "perhaps" list. Whenever an idea occurs to you of something you may want to do in a particular role, put it on a "perhaps" list for that role. Writing it here does not mean that it is a goal or a commitment; it is simply input to be considered in future planning. Writing it down diffuses the anxiety and distraction because it is duly noted and immediately accessible for future consideration.

Then, as you organize your week, you can quickly review your "perhaps" list as well as your long-term goals in each role. Each item on the list can be evaluated in context and perspective and, based on its comparative value, it can either be incorporated as a goal for the week, kept on the "perhaps" list for future reconsideration, or discarded as not really that important.

"Perhaps" lists provide an orderly framework for capturing and integrating insights and ideas in each role area. You may want to more fully implement the principle of ORDER by developing a notation to differentiate between short-term and long-term or lifestyle ideas, or to indicate those things that genuinely are "to do."

5. SET PRINCIPLE-BASED GOALS

*Hundreds of books have been written and pep talks given on the subject of goals. Goals have been inspected, dissected, and resurrected until we probably feel we know them inside-out. "A good goal is measurable, specific, time bound...etc." And we all know that the most important ingredient in setting and achieving goals is **self-control**. Right?*

*I suggest that, more than **self-control** successfully setting and achieving meaningful goals is a function of **self-release.***

*There is a basic difference in the fundamental thinking pattern between people who see human behavior from a perspective of **control** and those who see it from a perspective of **release**. If you have a control perspective, you basically assume that people have to be controlled, managed, or carefully supervised if they are to produce or perform well. If your perspective is one of release, your fundamental assumption is that, given the freedom, opportunity and support, people will bring out the highest and best within them and accomplish great things.*

The way you see others in terms of control or release is probably a reflection of the way you see yourself. If you have a control perspective, you assume you have to exercise strict control over yourself if you want to accomplish anything. If you have a release perspective, you see your primary facilitating task as creating the conditions under which your inner capacity can be released.

I suggest that, while we may achieve a degree of specific, measurable, identifiable success through self-control (and we've learned to be comfortable with that kind of success), quantum growth and change come principally through self-release.

*Basically, we release our capacity by **alignment**, by creating goals that are in line with, or grow out of, our mission, our values and principles. The greater the alignment, the more energy and capacity we release.*

One of the best ways I know to assure alignment, particularly on yearly or long-term goals, is to answer the following three questions:

1. WHAT? - What is it I want to accomplish? What are the results I want to achieve? (We're in agreement with most goal-setting theory here, focusing on results.)

2. WHY? - Why do I want to do it? (Here's the real difference, and the real release. **The key to motivation is motive.**) Is it in harmony with my deepest values and beliefs? Is it in harmony with my mission?

3. HOW? - What steps or strategies will I use to accomplish my goal? But, more fundamentally—What key principles will empower me to accomplish my purpose?

We often get so busy, so extrinsically controlled, that we work on the "goals" that are before us without ever really connecting them to our deepest values and purposes. We set **practice-based goals**, and we feel duty-bound to develop sufficient self control to achieve them, to endure to the end, to crawl battered and bruised over the finish line, if it's the last thing we do.

As a result, we fail to tap our deep energy sources, our convictions, our experiences. We're working against ourselves, not sure, deeply, why (or even **if**) we want to accomplish a particular goal. The commitments we make in a moment of enthusiasm often do not have sufficient sustaining power to carry us all the way to successful achievement of our goals. Then, when we fail to keep our commitments, we undermine our personal integrity.

It's not too hard to see why we sometimes become cynical about the goal-setting process. Repeatedly failing to achieve the goals we set or feeling we have to beat ourselves with a stick to accomplish things we have no deeply identifiable reason for doing can wear us out.

By dealing with the WHAT-WHY-HOW issues, we create the connection that plugs us in to our own high energy source. Because our goals are linked to our deepest values and desires, we are highly **motivated** to achieve them. Because their realization is based on principles, we are **empowered** to achieve them.

WHAT is direction; WHY is motivation; HOW is empowerment.

For example, if you wanted to buy a home, your goal analysis might go something like this:

WHAT—I want to buy a nice, comfortable family home.

WHY—We are expecting a child. One of my most important roles is as a husband and father, and in that role, I value providing a sense of security and physical comfort for my family.

*HOW—**Principle:** The fundamental principle that will empower me to achieve this goal is SUBORDINATION.*

*   **Application:** *I will postpone the stereo I wanted to buy, continue to drive the car I have for a while and do without other things so that I can put money toward the home.*

*   **Application:** *I will immediately begin to deposit 10% of my income each pay day into an account for a down payment.*

Many people would set as a "goal" one of the practice-bound applications I have suggested above. But a practice-bound application has no life in and of itself. Commitment without connection to values and missions is a tree without roots. It simply can't get the constant nourishment needed to grow and bear fruit.

*Principle-based goals release tremendous capacity and creativity within us. They do not exclude specific, measurable, time-bound commitments when they are useful. But the focus is on **principle** and **motive**, not on **activity**.*

Principle-based goals empower us with a MacGyver mentality, opening our minds to unexpected opportunities, to new ways of accomplishing objectives. We become free to pick and choose, to create and to put together elements of our environment to move us light-years ahead in new and exciting ways.

As we organize each week, we not only draw sustaining strength from reviewing our objectives, motives and principles of empowerment, but we are looking for other creative ways to move ahead. In moving toward the goal of buying a home, for example, we would not only be empowered to move confidently toward our goal in the midst of a wide range of choices and applications; we would also be looking for opportunities to find other creative ways to save money, to attend home shows, to go to the library and do some research on interior design, to create with our spouse a common vision of what we want a home to be. We would be empowered on a daily basis to recognize opportunity we had no way to predict. We would be creating the condition for meaningful spontaneity in our lives.

Principle-based goals can be used sometimes even on a weekly basis to achieve some of our most important objectives that simply cannot be crammed into the traditional goal-setting mode. If I want to improve my relationship with my teenage daughter, for instance, I could set aside a specific two hours on Saturday afternoon to spend time with her and listen empathically. But she may not want to talk on that particular day. I may have to sit there for two hours waiting for her to say something so I can communicate to her that I understand. Or her friends may call and ask her to go out for some pizza and leave me staring at the wall.

But if my goal is principle-based, reflects the values in my mission statement, and is connected to my role as a father, when I do my weekly organizing, I might simply put her name on my list of "today's priorities" for Monday. And then I watch for opportunity. If nothing happens on Monday, I draw an arrow on that line across to Tuesday. If nothing happens on Tuesday, I draw it on across to Wednesday. It's on my mind. I'm looking for creative ways to do it. And I can see what's happening in my week with regard to it.

Then, on Thursday, when I'm reading the paper and she comes in and wants to talk, I have the motivation to push my paper—not my daughter—aside. Here's opportunity. The time is right. It's what I really want to do. It's important. It's deeply connected to my values and my mission. It's my goal.

Principle-based goals help to move us into Quadrant II. As we review our long-term principle-based goals in each role when we organize the week, our minds are poised to think in terms of importance and opportunity. We can effectively evaluate the things on our "perhaps" list and coordinate goals with "to do's." We can find creative ways each week to move ahead, and by taking one bite at a time, we can eventually integrate anything we choose into our life process.

CHAPTER

The Action Connection

"On a clear day, you can see forever..."

But it's Tuesday

and the phone is ringing

and your secretary's late

and you just spilled ink on your brand new tie

and your boss just called a meeting for four o'clock

and your wife phoned to ask you to pick up some milk on the way home and you calmly walk over to open the window and yell, **"WHERE IN THE UNIVERSE IS QUADRANT II?"**

As we pointed out in Chapter One, it's a truly rare day that is the exact incarnation of a planning page. There are always currents exerting force on us from a variety of different directions. But we can navigate successfully and **we can do what we really want to do**. It just takes the final connection...the ACTION CONNECTION...to close the gap between our inner values and any given moment in time.

Let's look again for a minute at Lewin's Force Field Analysis and examine what we have already done to some of the powerful currents that usually get us off course.

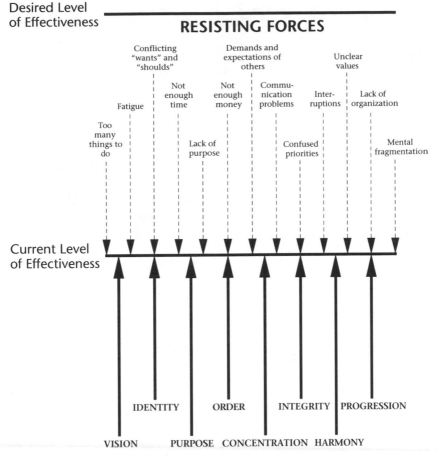

Desired Level of Effectiveness

RESISTING FORCES

Current Level of Effectiveness

IDENTITY   ORDER   INTEGRITY | PROGRESSION

VISION   PURPOSE   CONCENTRATION   HARMONY

DRIVING FORCES

It's easy to see we've made tremendous headway in weakening resisting forces as well as strengthening driving ones. Writing a personal mission statement has greatly dissipated the forces of too many things to do, conflicting wants and shoulds, the expectations and demands of others, confused priorities, lack of purpose and unclear values. Identifying our roles and goals and organizing on a weekly basis have further weakened those forces in addition to powerfully affecting lack of organization and mental fragmentation in our lives.

In addition, our increasing Quadrant II activities have helped us move out of other quadrants in our lives. We recognize the pseudo urgency of Quadrant III and are learning how to say "no." Because of better management on our part, we find fewer Quadrant I crises in our lives. And we feel good about what we're doing. We plan our growth, development and re-creation. We seldom feel the need to run to Quadrant IV.

Still, life is a moving, flowing thing. Currents arise that tend to alter our determined course.

The ACTION CONNECTION is that final link between your deepest values and your daily actions. It is based on the principles of PURPOSE, CONCENTRATION, and INTEGRITY, and the key strategies are **meaningful daily planning** and **asking the "important" question**.

When you completed your weekly organizing, you will remember you did not have your Weekly Worksheet completely filled. The important appointments and priorities for the week were entered, but there was still some blank space.

Each day you need to take a few moments and plan that day. As you do so, because of your weekly organizing, it is always in the context of what you determined, in a moment of clarity, was most important for you to do. Now, as you face the actual day, you can review the commitments you made, noting appointments and time-sensitive priorities in the scheduled space on the bottom and other things which could be done at any time during the day in the space for "Today's Priorities" on the top. You can fill in other things you feel you need to plan for the day, always working to be as accurate as possible in your estimate of what you can realistically accomplish in one day.

Give some indication of the priority status of each item on your "Today's Priorities" list, either by using management consultant Alan Lakien's ABC method (assign each item an A, B, or C, depending on importance, and always be working on A's), or by simply numbering them in order. I personally prefer the numbering method because it forces me to make very specific priority decisions.

I highly recommend then, that you go back over the items on the day's plan, including both scheduled and listed items, and identify the single most important thing to be done that day, either by circling it or by marking it with an asterisk. Make certain, if at all possible, that you do that thing. If the nature of the day is such that nothing else gets done, you have the satisfaction of knowing that you did the one thing that mattered most.

MONDAY
Today's Priorities
1. *Budget analysis*
5. *Personnel forms*
3. *Product brief*
2. *Call R & Sons*
4. *Meeting agenda*
Appointments/Commitments
8
9   *Long-range planning* *
10
11 *Interview J.J.*
12 *Lunch*
1
2
3   *Doctor Grahme*
4
5
6
Evening *Scout meeting*

When the day's planning and prioritizing are complete, then you can proceed to live the moments...**moments of truth**.

As you do so, you know you have planned the most important things to the best of your ability. And you also know that you are not omniscient. So, hopefully, you have planned, as I always do, in pencil. Nobody ever said that 6:30 in the morning you would somehow be able to predict everything that will happen in the course of the day. But you are a principle-centered, connected Quadrant II time manager. You know you are constantly trying to do what is most **important**. All you have to do in a moment of truth is answer the "important" question: "What is really **important** now?"

Suppose you go through the morning having successfully accomplished the first two items on your list of "Today's Priorities." Then you come to the point where you have an appointment scheduled with yourself to do some long-range planning, which you have identified as your most important task of the day. At that particular moment, you may not have the vision that was with you in the moment of clarity when you planned the week. You may feel forces acting on you to move you from your determined course. Opening or responding to the mail may suddenly seem more appealing, or you may think of something you need to talk over with an associate. The seemingly urgent may threaten to overpower the truly important. This is a moment of truth. If you ask the "important" question—"What is really **important** now?"—and act with integrity, you will keep your commitment and put a deposit in your personal integrity account. You concentrate your time and energies and move yourself further into Quadrant II.

As you continue through the day, an unexpected opportunity may arise. Perhaps a potential client calls just after lunch and asks if you can provide some information for a vital decision-making meeting at 3:00. Again, you ask the "important" question: "What is **important** now?" If the new opportunity is genuinely more in harmony with your values than what you had planned, you can change with integrity and make another deposit in your personal integrity account. You may be able to reschedule what you had originally planned for another time.

A real Quadrant I crisis, such as machine breakdown or a call that your daughter has been injured in an automobile accident, may arise later in the day. To respond to the important and truly urgent in one of your roles would be congruent with your inner values, and, again, you act with integrity by handling the crisis.

As you continue through the afternoon, you may come to a 4:00 appointment with your doctor. Because this is a "time-sensitive" priority, while it is important at 4:00, it has no priority at 6:00 (unless you're still waiting in the doctor's office). If you have not been able to accomplish your highest priorities for the day and the appointment is not critical, you may want to reschedule it. On the other hand, if it is an appointment you waited two months to get, if you are in danger of a heart attack, or if it is a Quadrant II health investment which carries high priority, you may want to keep the appointment and reschedule your other plans.

Acting based on what is **important** instead of **reacting** based on what is seemingly **urgent** gives you the freedom to make priority decisions on a daily basis with peace and confidence.

At the end of the day, the evaluation question is not, "Have I done everything on my plan?" It is, instead, "Have I acted with integrity to accomplish what was truly most important today?" If the answer is "YES," then you've done it! The important rather than the apparently urgent has determined your course. Your daily actions were firmly connected to your deepest values. You've lived one day of your life doing exactly what you really wanted to do.

STAYING ON TARGET

Making "important" decisions effectively is a skill that comes with practice. Each day, as you encounter new challenges, opportunities and priority decisions, you feel the frustration of **values in conflict**. The conflict may be external, meaning that your personal values come into conflict with those of someone else. Or it may be internal, meaning that one of your values is in conflict with another. Resolving these conflicts is a daily challenge, and I would like to suggest a strategy I feel is extremely helpful in making "important" decisions and staying on target. This strategy is adapted from a metaphor used extensively by my colleague, Stephen R. Covey.

When you feel a sense of frustration and your mind starts to run around in circles as you search for answers, stop for a minute and ask yourself just what circles you're running around in.

There is the Circle of Concern, the large circle that encompasses everything that reaches your awareness and about which you have some feeling. This may include a goal you want to set for improvement in a particular role, your son's plans for the weekend, offensive magazines on display in a neighborhood convenience store, the President's foreign policy decisions or the possibility of nuclear war. Although these things are valid concerns, you may or may not be able to really affect them. Your ability to do so is determined by whether or not they also fall into a smaller circle within your Circle of Concern called the Circle of Influence.

Your Circle of Influence defines the area of concern in which you can actually make a difference. While you may not be able to make the world safe from the threat of nuclear war, you can do what is necessary to set and achieve a meaningful goal in your life. In addition, you may have a good relationship with your son and be in a position to influence his week-end plans. Perhaps you belong to a Citizens for Decency committee or hold a position of responsibility in your local government and can effectively influence the standards for public display of obscene material in your community. Your Circle of Influence defines the concerns you have that you can do something about. But even this circle does not answer the question of whether or not the concern is something you **should** do something about.

In the center of your Circle of Influence is your Center of Focus. It is here that the things you are concerned about, that are within your ability to influence, **and that are in harmony with your deepest values and your mission** are found. This is the center of your target of personal effectiveness, the "bull's eye" of the effective management of your time and resources.

Every time you hit the center of that target, you maximize your time, talent and energy investment. Every time your aim is off and you land in some other circle, your personal effectiveness score takes a dive. When you hit your Circle of Concern, you basically waste time worrying about things you have no ability to control or affect. When you hit your Circle of Influence, you may do some good. But what you do may be at the expense of something better. And when something good takes the place of something better, that which is good becomes waste.

Interestingly, as you concentrate your life within your Center of Focus, your Circle of Influence automatically increases. You find in your growing personal strength the ability to affect more people and circumstances in positive ways. Your Circle of Influence may eventually expand to the point where it begins to fill your Circle of Concern, empowering you to affect even far reaching issues, such as the threat of nuclear war.

In addition, your Center of Focus provides the lens through which you see the world. If your focus is on financial gain, you tend to see the world in terms of money. **If you focus on your highest values and noblest purposes, you tend to see the world as an opportunity for noble accomplishment.**

Aiming at your Center of Focus is a function of setting principle-based goals that are in direct alignment with your values and mission, as we discussed in the special section on "Timely Tips from Quadrant II." As you review these goals each week and evaluate all the ideas and insights you have recorded on your "perhaps" list in that context, it becomes easy to zero in on most important things and to aim your effort in the right direction.

Principle-based goals also make it easier to stay in your Center of Focus on a daily basis, because **the key to motivation is motive**. Your reasons for accomplishing your goals are connected to your deepest values.

As you deal with decisions concerning how to spend your time and energy and with the forces in your life that tend to get you sidetracked or weaken your connections, keep the visualization of this target in mind. When unexpected opportunities arise or the seemingly urgent threatens to overpower the important, aim for the bull's eye.

Then when value conflicts arise, determine where on the target they fall. External conflicts may fall anywhere on the target and, to resolve them, you need to identify their location and determine what, if anything, you can do. Internal conflicts are always within your Center of Focus and can be resolved by **determining which value is higher** or by **finding a viable third alternative.** Let me give you a few examples.

Suppose you work for a company that has just purchased some lower quality parts to supply to your customers. You feel that the company is basically good, but, in the face of financial pressure, they took advantage of a good buy on an inferior product. The conflict of value between you and the company is within your Circle of Concern, but not within your Circle of Influence. You are not really in a position to do anything about the product and, if it came right down to it, you feel the company would terminate you before they would change their decision about the parts.

But there is also a value conflict within your Center of Focus...the conflict within yourself. On one hand, you value your job. On the other hand, you value your personal integrity and your relationship with your customers. To represent the parts as being of the same quality you have always provided would violate that value. But if you explain the difference to your customers, you will probably lose business and perhaps even your job.

To resolve the conflict, you have to **choose which value is more important to you** and either provide the part as you always have or tell the customers and take whatever consequences may come. This is a difficult situation, but by understanding your options, you can make your decision in harmony with your highest values and strengthen your connections in the process.

There are many instances in which value conflicts can more agreeably be solved by a **third alternative**. Suppose for example, that you own and operate a motel. Consumer surveys indicate that your business would increase significantly if you provided in-room movies for your guests. But the only economical cable service in your area is one that shows pornographic films on a regular basis.

This value conflict is within your Center of Focus. You are concerned, the decision is yours to make, and it affects your personal and professional value connections. On one hand, you value your business and want to please the customers. But spreading pornography violates your values of personal decency and community responsibility.

In this case, you might search for a third alternative. You might research until you discover a video company that installs VCRs in the rooms for a reasonable fee and provides a variety of movies which could be checked out by credit card from a vending machine. By agreement, you could select the movies made available to your customers.

For another example, suppose your boss comes to you on Friday with an important project he wants you to complete by Monday morning. Again, you are addressing a conflict within your Center of Focus. You value your job and your relationship with your boss, but you also value the weekend time with your family.

A third alternative would be to approach one of your co-workers about the possibility of staying late and working with you that night, in return for which you would be prepared to do the same for him on his next big project. Then you could both enjoy weekends at home.

Third alternatives are often the best way to resolve values in conflict. But there are times when there are no viable third alternatives and you simply have to determine which value is more important and act on it.

Keeping on target puts you in charge of your frustrations, your decisions, and the way you spend your time and energy. It provides the focus to maximize your efforts and the lens through which you see the world. It gives you a tool to help answer "important" questions effectively and to make meaningful deposits in your personal integrity account during moments of truth.

Increasing the Pace and the Peace

We now find ourselves ´at the point where we want to address the question that most time management courses focus on: how to get more done in less time. This, basically, is a question of **efficiency**. Now, **efficiency**, in and of itself, enables you to do **more** things, but it does not ensure that you are doing the **right** things, even when you "prioritize" the things you have to do. If you are not headed in the right direction, efficiency will only help you get to the wrong place faster.

That's why "connections" are so vitally important. As a connected Quadrant II time manager, you can now approach the question of efficiency with the fundamental difference that gives it meaning. Your "connections" enable you to put **efficiency** in a framework of **effectiveness**. The things you are trying to do more of are directly and deeply connected to your innermost values.

So as you now incorporate strategies of efficiency, you get to the right place faster. Headed in a consciously determined direction, you trade in your car for a jet.

My study of time management through the years has brought me in contact with a vast array of ideas to improve efficiency. In the process of synthesizing those ideas and analyzing my own experience, I have identified ten basic strategies which I feel are in harmony with the timeless principles we have discussed and are supremely effective in enabling people to get more important things done in less time.

1. GET BETTER AT WHAT YOU DO A LOT OF

If you draw back and look at the way you spend your time, you will probably find there are certain things within your chosen roles that you spend a lot of time doing. Focusing efficiency improvement efforts on those things will bring great returns.

Take reading, for example. Proficiency in your job may require that you assimilate a great deal of written material on a regular basis. If you spend several hours reading and average 300 to 400 words a minute with a 60% retention level, how much more efficient could you be by increasing that to several thousand words a minute with a 90% retention level? A Quadrant II investment in a speed reading course could enable you to do that.

Perhaps you have to remember names for customer service. Learning how to do that effectively through available books or courses can free your time and mental energies for other things and can significantly influence the positive reaction others have toward you.

There are also excellent resources available to help you handle paperwork, phone calls, or meetings with greater dispatch.

If you travel a lot, learn how to pack, what to pack, how to handle affairs at the airport to make the right connections, where to stay, what seat to reserve on the airplane so you can work more effectively en route, and how to keep accurate reports and expense records as you go so you won't be behind when you return.

Refine skills you need to use frequently, such as selling or marketing, and analyze your effectiveness. Communication skills, parenting skills and homemaking skills are rich areas for improvement. Research and develop those techniques that will bring you greater results for the time you spend.

2. BE WHERE YOU ARE

A woman who tries to plan a committee meeting and handle the needs of her preschoolers at the same time may wind up with peanut butter and jelly on the agenda and a well-deserved feeling of ineffectiveness in both jobs. It is possible to handle several areas of responsibility well, but it is critical to be able to devote your time to the focus of the moment, to "be where you are."

Leaving your work at the office frees you to be a far more effective spouse and parent at home. Focusing completely on the person you are talking with expedites the business at hand and makes that individual feel your deep, personal interest in him and his concerns. Concentrating your mental energies on what you are doing instead of on the twenty other things you aren't doing has powerful impact on the effectiveness of the results.

As you focus your mental and emotional energy and your physical presence in any moment, you make that moment rich and full and vitally productive. What you can accomplish in that focused moment of time far exceeds the results of effort that is fragmented, either from without or within.

3. SYNERGIZE

"Synergy" is a term used to describe the phenomenon that occurs when two or more things combine in such a way that the whole is greater in effect than the sum of the individual effects. My colleague, Stephen R. Covey, identifies synergy as one of the "Seven Habits of Highly Effective People" because of its powerful result in creative interpersonal problem-solving. The ideas and solutions generated by the interaction of several individuals far exceed the sum of what the individuals could come up with on their own.

In the area of time management, I define the word "synergy" to describe the results achieved when two or more objectives are accomplished by a single activity. For example, you may be able to meet your goals in the areas of exercise and building your relationship with your teenage daughter by taking her out for a game of tennis. You may be able to inspect a factory, train a new assistant and hold his performance review by taking that assistant with you to the factory and discussing his performance on the way.

Anytime you can combine several objectives into one activity, you dramatically increase the value of that activity.

4. SEGMENT

When you have a big project to do, such as organize a file, write a report or plan a presentation, the mere size of the endeavor tends to be overwhelming. It seems easier to procrastinate and worry about it than to jump in and do it.

I have found that many highly productive individuals do not view a big project as a solid entity. Rather, they tend to look at it as a structure comprised of several smaller units or segments. As they plan time to accomplish the project, they plan it in several independent blocks. A research project, for example, might be divided into a two-hour block for planning and locating resource materials, several two-hour blocks for reading and taking notes, a half-day block for assimilating and outlining, a half-day block for writing the original draft, a one-hour block for proof reading and correcting, and a two-hour block for completing the final draft.

Segmentation allows you to divide big projects into conquerable parts and handle them one at a time. Now available on many microcomputers are project scheduling packages which break large tasks down and organize them, bringing people, resources and schedules together in ways that save tremendous amounts of time.

5. START AND FINISH STRONG

As any athlete knows, a poor start or a weak finish will never win the race. It is the discipline of running a good race, start to finish, that brings the victory.

In accomplishing tasks, a strong start includes preparation: having objectives and results identified, tools and materials ready, people notified, physical facilities arranged and adequate time scheduled. A strong start also includes a significant investment up front in terms of time and effort. If you tackle a massive part of the task at the beginning, you get a good feel for the project as a whole and you experience a real sense of success in having done the difficult first.

The enthusiasm generated at the beginning of a task unfortunately makes for more strong starters than strong finishers.

There is a tendency to leave the last few things undone, to not quite finish a project. This forces you to return to the task at a later time when your objectives and ideas are not so clear, which decreases your effectiveness and increases the time demands of the task. Exercising the discipline necessary to just "gut it out" and see a task to its completion makes a significant deposit in your personal integrity account.

Strong starts are also vital to the implementation of successful daily planning. Most of us, when confronted with a number of tasks for the day, tend to get the little ones out of the way first so that we can then concentrate on the "big" one. The main problem with this approach is that we use our freshest, most creative time on the easiest tasks. This leaves us with decreasing enthusiasm, dwindling time and mounting anxiety to apply to the most difficult task.

If your priorities for a Saturday at home are to clean out a messy garage, repair your son's bike, plant some flowers and mow the lawn, you may be tempted to get everything else out of the way first so that you can really "get down to business" when you get to that messy garage. But if you devote your early morning hours to that big job when your mind and muscles are rested, it will probably go much faster. The feelings of confidence and success you gain from getting that major job out of the way give you more energy to complete the smaller tasks. And organizing the garage will undoubtedly make it easier for you to find the tools you need to get the other jobs done faster.

At the office, paperwork, phone calls and a wide variety of minutia tend to eat up your fresh, creative morning time if you let them. So put them on "hold" and attack your big priorities first. Your increase in productivity will be phenomenal. But don't let the tremendous feeling of success cause you to sit back and gloat for the rest of the day. Finish strong...handle the paperwork, the phone calls and the minutia in your less intense afternoon time.

One effective way to inspire a strong finish is to set up a Quadrant II incentive for yourself, such as a relationship-building or re-creational activity, when the task is complete.

6. INSULATE AND ISOLATE

Wires designed to carry an electric energy force are "insulated" so that the energy will flow along a prescribed path and reach its destination with full power. The insulation assures that energy will not be diverted along the way.

As you direct your energies in a determined path, particularly in the area of Quadrant II activities, you may find you sometimes need "insulation" to utilize your full power. Insulators might include a secretary, a closed door, older children to take care of younger ones and answer the phone at home, or even the way you communicate with others, letting them know, politely and firmly, that you are focused and busy.

There may be times when "isolation" is necessary for the accomplishment of your objectives. You may need to get away from the office and go to the library or another location where you can be alone and uninterrupted to focus on high leverage work.

7. ORGANIZE AND CATEGORIZE

If you find you spend a lot of your time looking for things, set aside some Quadrant II time to get organized. "A place for everything and everything in its place" may sound trite, but efficiency demands organization.

One really effective way to organize current information is by roles. As already mentioned, a "perhaps" list in each role area provides a very effective way to keep track of possible goals and activities. Professional information can be filed in a file drawer set up according to your job roles. There might be a folder for each role (perhaps even color coded for faster identification), and then subdivisions for more specific information within each role. Projects in process can also be organized by role and then transferred to the file drawer when completed. Family information, such as gift ideas, clothing sizes or parenting goals can be organized in a file drawer, 3X5 card file or in your personal planning tool under the appropriate role. Your own *plans for personal development, list of books to read, record of exercise or "wish" list can be filed under your role as an individual.*

You might also organize notes in the same way. People tend to take notes frequently, which is handy at the time, but becomes dysfunctional when the time comes to retrieve the information. If the notes are filed in a particular role area, the mental association makes retrieval quick and easy.

The fundamental advantage in organizing according to your roles is that the organization follows your own mental process. Often trying to follow elaborate filing systems that someone else has devised almost defeats the purpose, unless you happen to have the same mental framework as the system developer.

8. SIMPLIFY

When you have a task to do, cut it down mentally to the bare essentials. You may want to add the non-essentials after consideration, but first take stock of what is absolutely necessary to get the job done.

One acquaintance of mine never wanted to invite friends over to her home. She deeply wanted the companionship of others, but felt that having company required the equivalent of spring cleaning the house, providing a banquet for the guests, and having her family and herself groomed to look like they had just stepped out of a fashion magazine.

When she realized the essentials—being together and having a good time—she discovered that she could vacuum the front room, send the kids out to play, serve hot dogs and potato salad on paper plates and actually enjoy being with her guests...and the sky wouldn't fall!

How many of the meetings you attend are really necessary? How much of what goes on at those meetings is really essential? How many letters do you dictate when a two sentence memo would do the job? How many policies and procedures are vital to the success of your company?

*How much time could you gain by simplifying the things you do? Or the things you **have**? If you spend a great deal of time just taking care of physical possessions that really do not fit in* *with your roles or contribute to your goals, get rid of them. There are better ways to spend that time.*

Remember in simplifying not to cut things too thin. Simplification should always eliminate the excess, not the essentials.

9. DROP DISTRACTIONS

When you are on a particular task and a distraction comes along, just drop it. I have seen one very effective individual literally do just that. Sometimes when he is working on a project, he finds himself going after a report, which leads to a book, which leads to a different question which leads him off on another track. When he realizes his distraction, he literally drops the books on the floor and goes back to his project, returning at a later time to pick up the books. This rather dramatic mental cue reminds him forcefully to avoid distractions that draw him away from a task.

10. CLARIFY EXPECTATIONS UP FRONT

If you analyze the time you spend working with other people, you will probably discover a sizable amount wasted in reclarifying instructions or agreements, re-doing things not done correctly the first time, repairing relationships damaged through misunderstanding, or simply working against uncertainty in terms of expected results.

As a manager, parent, or leader, it's often easy in such situations to see other people as incompetent and to develop the attitude that it's easier to do something yourself than to work with others.

"But Dad! I did what you said!" your nine year-old son says with a hurt expression in his eyes. " I cleaned the garage." As you look at the boxes stacked haphazardly by the wall and the only dirt-free surface in the center of the garage floor, you question the sanity of the teacher that graduated him from kindergarten.

But something in that expression tells you that he really did think he accomplished what you wanted him to do. In his mind, he fulfilled the assignment. And he expected you to be pleased.

While "clean the garage" meant one thing to you—

garbage carried out, boxes organized, tools in place, floor swept (including the corners) and burned-out light bulbs replaced—it meant something entirely different to a nine year-old boy. As a result, you're both disappointed, the work experience is negative and the relationship becomes strained.

The consequences of unclear expectations are not always as easy to see in working with adults who have learned to live with repeating, re-doing and relating on a surface level to protect tender feelings. But they're there, and they're responsible for many hours, days and even weeks of wasted time. They become a major cost in the industrial setting.

*The maxim **"you make time if you take time"** has one of its greatest applications in this area of interdependent human interaction. Take time to empathically listen to other people involved in interdependent effort. Make sure you know where they're coming from—what's really important to them, what they see in their minds in terms of what constitutes a job "well done," what responsibility they really accept. Take time to work out "win/win" agreements that are mutually satisfying and beneficial. Take time to specify desired results, guidelines and parameters, and to set up accountability.*

Clarifying expectations is an important, non-urgent high-leverage Quadrant II activity. When you don't make expectations clear, the resulting misunderstanding and inadequate performance frequently throw you into Quadrant I, trying to meet what have become urgent deadlines in an atmosphere of strained relationships.

When you do take the time to clarify expectations from the beginning, you provide the foundation for successful interdependent effort, and you free time down the road for better things than re-doing what already could have been done.

*Now I entitled this section "Increasing the Pace **and the Peace**" for an important reason. I know that these ten strategies will dramatically increase how much you can do in a given amount of time. But I also know that, no matter how efficient you become at what you do, your mental abilities are such that **you will always be aware of more than you can possibly do**. You can continue to build your ability to do more and more, but you always do whatever you do at the expense of not doing something else.*

You can, for instance, continue to work on a project into the evening, but you do so at the cost of time with your family. You can continue to work on a project into the night, but you do so at the cost of revitalizing rest for your mind and body. And if your focus on doing more and more blinds you to the deeper purpose behind the doing, your connections will be broken and the inner peace of knowing your life is in harmony with your deepest values will be gone.

Remember again the maxim: **"you can do anything you want, but not everything."**

Keep the principle of HARMONY in your life. Successfully conducting your life is like conducting a beautiful symphony; when the song is written in four-four time, you simply can't get more than four beats to a measure! Even the incorporation of these ten strategies into your life can be done in an orderly and harmonious manner by selecting one strategy at a time and setting specific goals for implementation during your weekly organizing.

Quantity is important, but not at the expense of **quality** in your life. Remember to keep **efficiency** in its place...within the framework of **effectiveness**. And keep your "connections" intact, so that the things you are doing more of are directly connected to your innermost values.

CHAPTER

The Interconnection

A friend of mine who is now a published author recently shared with me an incident from her earlier experience. At the time, she was a busy mother and would-be writer. She was devastated one day to walk into the book store and see on the shelves a book that had been written by an acquaintance with whom she had a past close association.

"I felt so angry," she explained. "How in the world could she have done it? She had a husband, kids, a home to take care of. Where did she get the time to do something like that?

"The longer I looked at that book, the madder I got. I thought, 'She probably hires a baby-sitter to take care of the kids. I'll bet her husband is rolling in money. They probably eat out every night so she doesn't have to fix dinner. And she's got so much energy. She's probably never been sick a day in her life. There's no way she could have written that book if she had to handle the challenges I have.'

"As my angry thoughts ran on, I thought of other things I never had time for. Suddenly, every book on that shelf seemed to jump out and yell, 'Why haven't you read me?' It wasn't long before I felt like a hopeless, incompetent, victimized, frustrated mess. I was furious with my 'perfect' friend and with the people and circumstances I felt were responsible for my own stagnant situation.

"I went out to the car and sat there for a few minutes just thinking. Somewhere deep inside I knew my response was way out of proportion. I knew there had to be some underlying reason for the way I felt, so I decided to sort it all out. I tried to just let go of all the negative, blaming, angry reactions and look honestly into my own heart.

"I had one of those wonderful, painful flashes of light that suddenly lets you see everything for what it is. I wasn't really mad at my friend. She simply had some things in her life that I didn't...some things I knew I needed to have. I was seeing her accomplishments as a mirror of my own weaknesses. And, seeing myself in that mirror, I lashed out at the reflection.

"I knew she was a great mother. Mothering was a challenge for me, and I was seeing her tremendous patience and positive attitude as a foil to what I felt was my own incompetence. She managed her time to do meaningful and creative things outside the home. I knew I had a talent for writing too, but I simply had not been efficient enough in my other responsibilities to find the time to develop that talent.

"I was assuming financial ease on her part because I felt restricted by a weakness in money management. Some wrong decisions earlier in our marriage had put us in a position of debt. I felt that bondage kept me from doing a lot of things I wanted to do in life.

"My friend was healthy, but that wasn't the problem. The problem was that I knew I ought to exercise on a regular basis...and I didn't do it.

"If I had been doing the things in my own life I knew I ought to be doing, I never would have had those feelings in the first place. My friend's success would have been the joy it should have been to me.

"I knew I couldn't snap my fingers and suddenly change all those things in my life. But, at least, I knew the root of the problem was my own incongruence. And that was something, over a period of time, I could do something about."

My friend's experience revealed a very important truism: basically, **the approach you take in your relationship with others usually mirrors the relationship you have with yourself.** If your inner connections are intact, your interconnections are generally harmonious and rewarding. You feel good about yourself as a centered, worthwhile person who, given time and encouragement, will grow to fill the inner picture you have created. You tend to see others as individuals who also have important values and goals and treat them with the same respect you feel toward yourself. Because your personal integrity account is high, you approach situations with confidence. Even though you may be in a high pressure situation, your level of stress is generally low. Others see you as an authentic, genuine person and respond favorably to you.

When you are disconnected and your personal integrity account is in the red, your confidence level is low and your stress level is high. Others sense duplicity in you and respond to you in a guarded manner. If you feel you need to put constant restraints and controls on yourself to force you to live true to whatever inner feelings you may have, you tend to see others in a paradigm of control. You tend to treat them with suspicion, assuming if they are not constantly and closely supervised, they will immediately get off track.

One impactful aspect of this in the area of human relations is the self-fulfilling prophecy or the "Pygmalion effect." People tend to fulfill expectations. If you treat people as creative, worthwhile individuals who are moving in a positive direction in life, they tend to become just that.

If you treat them with a paradigm of control, they generally tend to need control. This is particularly obvious in the corporate society.

Research in the field of organizational behavior and industrial psychology has repeatedly indicated that the culture of any corporation is a reflection of the leadership of the corporation. There's the "control" culture where employees are seen as irresponsible, requiring constant supervision, never performing up to their potential, and ready to take off early or appropriate company supplies for personal use whenever the opportunity presents itself. This is the culture of suspicion and mistrust.

And then there's the "release" culture, where employees are seen as intelligent, creative individuals who, if given support, training, encouragement and involvement, will give the corporation their best and make great contributions to the company's success. This is the culture of respect.

I submit that the core issue involved in the difference is **connections**—whether or not the corporation leadership has established those personal **inner connections** that make effective **interconnections** possible.

A connected executive has a high personal integrity account. He trusts himself and tends to trust others, too.

He listens to his own inner guidance system and knows that what he hears is worthwhile. He listens, then, to others and recognizes that the ideas and viewpoints of others have value also.

In negotiations, he works for synergistic solutions that genuinely meet the needs of others as well as his own. He constantly seeks for third alternatives and better ways.

He sees differences as other approaches that may also be worthy of consideration.

Unfortunately, many organizations do not have the benefit of such inner-connected and inter-connected leadership. When a number of individuals with varying degrees of personal incongruency interact in a corporate society, the networks sometimes become so complex that the core problems become totally obscured. Time and money are poured into treating symptoms when no one has accurately diagnosed the fundamental underlying problem.

I remember one day several months ago, I picked up my home telephone to make an important call and put it to my ear, only to hear a series of terrible, loud static noises. I pressed several of the buttons a few times, wiggled the cord, hung up for a minute and tried again. The static was still there. I attempted to dial a number, but nothing happened. Finally, in desperation, I went to our neighbor's house to make my call and phone a repairman.

He was out within a few hours and quickly located the problem. Some men who had been working on the sewer on our street had cut a line, and a connection some 50 yards from my house was almost severed.

Now I could have taken that telephone apart, piece by piece; I could have replaced any number of parts; I could have even replaced the phone. But I still would not have solved the problem. The static in the phone itself was only a symptom of a much deeper problem...a broken connection.

Many of the symptoms that keep surfacing in survey after survey as "time management" problems in organizations have their roots in disconnections. They include such things as:

- too much "busy work"
- unimportant assignments
- excessive meetings
- long meetings
- interruptions
- failure to delegate
- excessive policies and procedures
- too much red tape
- poor organization
- lack of communication
- unnecessary correspondence
- office politics
- gossip at the water fountain

In order to solve what is perceived as "the problem," companies attempt to train their people in techniques of holding effective meetings, handling interruptions, delegation skills, communication skills and "time management." Now I believe skill training is great; the first suggestion I made in the preceding section to increase efficiency was to get better at what you do a lot of. That includes things like holding meetings, communicating and delegating.

But that suggestion was based on the assumption that what you do a lot of, you do by conscious choice, and that it is directly related to your chosen roles and your innermost values. To work on skills and techniques without a solid foundation of connections is merely to treat the symptoms of the problem and not the problem itself. And, while treating the symptoms may alter the situation somewhat, it does not solve the problem any more than replacing my telephone would have solved my problem at home. Disconnection is often at the bottom of such problems, creating static all along the line. Until it is diagnosed and treated, the symptoms will remain and reappear, time and time again.

Let's look at some of those organizational symptoms more closely. Take "busy work" for example. People without the intrinsic security of a connected life often tend to validate their self-worth by the number of concrete, tangible, measurable things they do. The number of letters sent out (whether or not they are necessary or meaningful), the number of phone calls made, the number of "to do's" checked off a list, the number of people contacted or trade journals read cover to cover determine the success of their day. These individuals may be very "busy," but, in terms of how their activities reflect their deepest values, may not be very effective at all. Incidentally, the same symptom surfaces in many other areas, most noticeably in social clubs, homes, and sometimes in service organizations.

Executives and supervisors often subconsciously justify their position of authority by providing busy work for others. Unimportant assignments that drain the time and energy of the work force tend to validate their feelings of self-worth. They appear to be effective; they keep their staff running all day every day. But how much of what is done contributes significantly to the purpose of the organization? And what could be done with that time and energy if it were more profitably used?

Let's look at excessive and lengthy meetings. How many of the meetings you attend are really necessary? How much is actually accomplished in those meetings? If you were to identify the results at the end of a particular meeting, would they justify the time spent?

The fact is that often people do not have their job roles clearly defined. The insecurity created by unclear expectations or lack of alignment of values, goals and strategies within the organization fosters confusion. Wanting to feel like a productive and contributing member of a team, they turn to the one thing that seems to validate that image...meetings. As long as they're meeting, as long as they're working together to solve the problems, they're productive and contributing...aren't they?

Of course, effective and necessary meetings are an integral part of a successful organization. But what percentage of our meetings actually are effective or necessary?

And what about organizational "red tape?" Let's look at an executive we'll call Jim. Jim has worked with his company for a number of years and, in the process, has accumulated quite a bit of important information about the company and its clients. But things are changing. The company has hired a number of new, younger employees and is redesigning its strategy. Jim's personal security comes from his job, not his connections, and he feels threatened.

As a result, he makes it difficult for new employees to have access to certain information they need. He maintains a tight control and insists on certain policies and procedures that make it necessary for them to come to him for information. In doing so, he further entrenches himself in his own niche in the organization and validates the importance of his job. But what is the cost to the organization?

How much policy and procedure is actually necessary in a company? And how much of it is the result of the "control" mentality...the result of disconnected leadership whose grasp for control and discipline is directed outward rather than inward?

As companies seek to resolve their problems with symptomatic skill training, they swat at flies instead of patching the hole in the screen door. Certainly, there are many areas in organizations where specialized skill training is needed. But think for a moment how different your work or even your home environment would be if every individual there were operating from a solid base of connections. What if the people you work or associate with had a clear understanding of their personal values and a written statement of their missions in life? What if they organized their time and resources each week to move them toward the fulfillment of those missions? What if they lived each day with integrity, being true to the best within them?

What if the members of your family were connected by a family mission statement of agreed upon values and goals? What if the company you work for had an organizational mission statement that represented the shared values and objectives of the people who work there? Would that affect many of the "problems" that consistently beset organizations?

I don't begin to pretend that connections provide the panacea to solve all the ills that afflict mankind. But I really do believe that a connected individual who has a deeper sense of who he is and where he's going works to solve whatever problems he encounters from a base of tremendous personal strength and understanding. There is a direct correlation between our **inner connections** and our **interconnections**. And connected individuals, working together with common purposes and clear expectations in home, business, community or any group endeavor, create a powerful synergy to facilitate progress and growth.

With that in mind, I believe that harmonious interconnections can best be achieved by doing the following things:

1. **Create harmonious inner connections first.**
Resolve the conflict between wants and shoulds in your

life. Identify your deepest values. Write your personal mission statement and define what you want to be and to do. Organize your vision in terms of roles and goals, translate it into daily action and act with integrity in moments of truth. Stay on target. Begin to see yourself as a congruent, worthwhile individual who, with time and encouragement, will turn that vision into realization.

2. **Look beyond the static.** When you have problems or conflict in your relationships with others, look deeper for the possible cause. Blaming, accusing, angry feelings toward others usually result from inner incongruity. The specific things you feel most negatively about in others can often give you insight into your own areas of disconnection within. Of course other people aren't perfect; they have problems and weaknesses and are often the victims of their own emotions. But you can handle interactions with them with calmness and confidence, you can get to the heart of the real issues, and you can resolve problems much more quickly if your inner connections are intact.

3. **Let respect govern your interactions with others.** Treat others as you want them to become...as you, yourself, want to become. By assuming the best, you bring out the best in others.

The INTERCONNECTION is based on the principle of HARMONY. Inner harmony precedes interactive harmony. And because we live in an interdependent society, **learning to live in harmony with others is just as essential as creating harmony within ourselves.**

CHAPTER

Quadrant II[3]

This is a test.

Suppose you have $10 which you can invest in one of four ways to bring the following returns:

Investment I	Investment II
You get your $10 back	You get $1,000
Investment III	**Investment IV**
You get $5 of your $10 back	You lose your $10

Think carefully. Which of the four investments would you make?

If you selected investments I, III, or IV, you might want to set this book down for a while and go have a lengthy conversation with your analyst.

If you chose investment II, I assume you like to receive a good return on your investments. I do, too. I like to receive a good return on my financial investments and I like to receive a good return when I invest my time. That's why investing time in Quadrant II makes so much sense.

With Quadrant I crisis investments, you usually just about break even. When you make Quadrant III pseudo-urgent investments, you may only lose a part of what you invest because they sometimes meet the priorities of others who are important to you. (Conscious investment in the real priorities of others is a Quadrant II relationship-building activity that brings great returns.) Quadrant IV not-urgent, not-important investments are basically a waste. But Quadrant II investments bring pay-offs in a big way. I quantify the return in my own mind with the symbol QII^3, or "Quadrant II to the third power." The investment often brings returns that can only be described in terms of significant increase.

I hope by now you recognize the increasing power that comes from writing a personal mission statement. A quality personal mission statement is a significant investment of time, but the benefits of this activity over a lifetime are incredible. Weekly organizing takes time— about 15 to 30 minutes a week. But, again, the returns far outweigh the investment. The strategies mentioned in Chapter Three to increase learning effectiveness are other examples of QII^3.

The Quadrant II activities I want to present now could best be introduced by the old story that is told of two men chopping trees in the forest. The first set a steady pace and worked all day without stopping. The second worked equally hard, but took a few minutes every hour, on the hour, to sit down and rest. At the end of the day, the second man had cut and stacked almost twice as much wood as the first.

The first man came to his co-worker and said, "I don't understand it. I have worked just as hard as you and I haven't even stopped to rest. You have rested every hour during the day. How is it possible that you have cut twice as much wood as I?"

The second man replied, "Yes, my friend, I have stopped to rest. But the thing you failed to notice is that each time I sat down, I sharpened my axe."

We sometimes work diligently, hour after hour, day after day, not realizing that the principal reason behind our painfully slow progress is little more than a dull blade. In these circumstances, the amount of time and energy we invest seems unreasonably high in proportion to the return, which is in direct opposition to the nature of Quadrant II effectiveness. But it's amazing what we can do when we take a little time to sharpen the axe.

A modernized version of this tale provides the basis for the seventh habit taught in the "Seven Habits of Highly Effective People" called "Sharpening the Saw." The section entitled "Sharpening the Saw" at the bottom of your Weekly Worksheet provides a place where you can plan a regular program of renewing activities in each of the four human dimensions—physical, mental, spiritual and social/emotional.

There are certainly a number of strategies that would appropriately accomplish the purpose of renewal, but my own search for Quadrant II effectiveness has led me to discover three activities which I believe to be supremely effective. These activities are so powerful because they are **synergistic**; they have pay-offs in more than one dimension.

I think it is a mistake to think of the four dimensions as independent; they are highly interconnected. Your physical health affects your mental attitude and vice-versa. Your spiritual congruency affects your emotions and the way you interact with others. Emotional health has a significant impact on physical health, and so on. There are many points of connection between the four dimensions.

I believe those synergistic activities that renew several dimensions at once are more effective in that the same investment accomplishes several interconnected purposes.

With that in mind, let me share with you the three activities that have significantly increased effectiveness for many others, as well as for myself.

WALKING

Imagine yourself outside on a bright, beautiful day. The sky is blue, the air is fresh, and the beauties of nature and life surround you. Maybe you are alone; maybe you are with your spouse or a friend. Perhaps you are on the beach, on a mountain-trail, or on the sidewalk in your neighborhood. And you walk...maybe a couple of miles, maybe more. You don't really think about the fact that you are reducing your blood pressure, increasing your energy, toning your muscles, stimulating your circulation and controlling your weight. You just know you feel great. You feel like you could tackle anything. And when you go back, you probably can.

Walking touches every dimension of the human personality. The physical benefits seem apparent. Although we have been literally flooded with information on the benefits of various forms of exercise, research keeps coming back to the time-proven value of the "daily constitutional." Distance, speed and frequency may affect the aerobic or weight control value of walking, but any walking, for any distance, at any speed on a regular basis brings returns in the physical dimension.

The mental benefits are significant. Walking allows you time to clear your mind and bring it to equilibrium. It gives you the opportunity to focus on a particular problem or concern without interruption. Writers, scientists, executives, people from all "walks" of life claim some of their greatest ideas and inspirations come when they are on foot.

When I speak of the spiritual dimension, I refer to the source of your values and identity. Whatever your philosophy or theology, there is a need to frequently connect with the innermost aspects of your self. Walking provides time for contemplation, time to connect in a very fundamental and essential way.

The social/emotional benefits are also great. My wife and I have had some of our most meaningful times of communication as we walk together in the evenings. We share, we listen to each other, we discuss our concerns away from telephones, doorbells and other people. I sometimes walk with one of our children and have some marvelous one-on-one time. Walking is a great relationship-building investment.

Emotions that may have resulted from the pressures and challenges of the day seem to dissipate into a feeling of calmness during a walk.

There are so many benefits to walking. I'm a great believer in the renewing value of donning my Rocksports and putting a few miles under my feet on a daily basis.

WRITING

Writing—specifically, keeping a daily journal—is another valuable high-leverage activity. This, too, is a time-proven practice with benefits in several dimensions.

The spiritual benefits include a daily opportunity to re-establish essential inner connections and to assess experience and performance in light of fundamental values. It also provides valuable personal feedback we have no other way of getting. As we review pages from our past, our view of ourselves is not limited by the only real awareness of the present moment.

Mentally, writing forces us to clarify and give solid expression to sometimes vague thoughts and feelings. It deepens our understanding and helps us separate the wheat from the chaff in our interactions with others. The moment of interaction may be clouded by circumstance or emotion, but the act of evaluating helps clarify what really happened and why.

Keeping a journal is a powerfully therapeutic emotional tool. Feelings that would otherwise be buried and left to fester are exhumed, examined and dealt with.

Excepting a direct connection to the physical dimension, keeping a daily journal touches every facet of human renewal.

READING AND LISTENING

I recently came across some research which indicates that most of today's high school graduates will have spent more time in front of the television than in the classroom, and that some 70% of them will never read another book, cover to cover, in their lives.

I believe being widely read is fundamental to the MacGyver mentality. The more you know, the more aware you are of timeless, self-validating, empowering principles and the more options you have open in any situation. I include "listening" with reading because, through modern technology, we have access to cassette tapes of talks, seminars, and even books from some of the greatest thinkers of our time and throughout history. What a marvelous investment of time to listen to a tape while you're walking or driving or doing any other activity that does not directly engage your mind.

When we talk about time management, we usually refer to the things we **do** in time. We could also take a look at what we **think** in time. From the perspective of the Time Management Matrix, we waste a lot of mental time in Quadrants III and IV on the seemingly urgent and the unimportant. Shifting your mind to Quadrant II is another monumental step toward effectiveness in your life.

Reading and listening do more than increase your mental power. They open important doors in the social/emotional dimension. You come in contact with some of the greatest minds that exist or have existed on this planet. Capturing and processing their ideas and experiences gives you a greatly increased respect for others. Vicariously experiencing the lives of characters in classical and quality modern literature provides emotional development beyond the sphere of your own personal experience. As you capture and process, you come in contact with many essential ideas which affect your own spiritual dimension.

Again, excepting a direct connection to the physical dimension, this activity affects every aspect of renewal.

These activities are applications of the principle of PROGRESSION. The time to implement these or other Quadrant II renewing activities is during weekly organizing. Set specific goals and make appointments with yourself or set up time zones to invest in renewing activities. As you plan and live through each day, keep your commitments with integrity. You'll be amazed at the quality and quantity of your performance when you take time to sharpen the saw.

CHAPTER

The Other Resource

I have an acquaintance whose family is very high on his list of values. His teenage son was having problems, struggling with some important decisions in his life. If there was ever a time he needed guidance and help, this was it.

My friend knew he needed to spend some quality time with the boy. He arranged to be away from his work for a few days, packed up the jeep and headed for the mountains. The setting was beautiful. They walked and fished and slept out under the stars. After a time, the boy began to talk, sharing his deep concerns with his Dad. It was a time of close communication and bonding, a time of making deep inner connections and good decisions that would impact the rest of a young life. In the process, my friend gained tremendous insight into the nature of the challenges his son was facing. He discovered things he could do, changes he could make, to be a better help to his boy.

If my friend had not been able to manage his resources to meet this critical need in his son's life, those important decisions would have been made under very different circumstances and could well have taken a much different turn.

I contrast my friend's situation to that of another man I know who also puts high priority on his family. He earnestly wants to be there for his children when they need him, but he is holding down two jobs to put bread on the table and pay off his debts. He hardly sees his family, and taking time off from work to spend with his son would be completely out of the realm of possibility.

In trying to accomplish the things that are really important to us, we basically have two resources we deal with every day: time and money. Our inability to manage either resource well shackles us in our effort to be effective.

So this chapter is about the "other resource"—money. It is not a detailed approach to money management, but is rather a brief overview of how the timeless and empowering principles and Quadrant II strategies we have already discussed can apply to the management of this vital resource.

To begin with, let's look at the way we spend money. Again we can refer to the quadrant matrix. Quadrant I spending is "urgent and important," including things such as payments, bills and immediate needs. Quadrant II spending is "important and not urgent," including future needs, savings and investments. Quadrant III "urgent but not important" spending would include unplanned, unnecessary impulse buying. And Quadrant IV "not urgent, not important" spending results from waste, bad judgment and expenditures that are out of harmony with your goals.

Again, most people spend their financial lives in Quadrants I and III, paying bills, meeting immediate needs and buying on impulse. And they never get ahead. Some Quadrant I spending is necessary. But Quadrant II is the Quadrant of Financial Freedom, the quadrant where we make significant strides toward meeting our important goals.

The same principles that enable us to manage our time effectively apply to the management of money.

VISION provides a wide range of alternatives for acquiring and using money. It enables us to see money in the context of values and purposes.

IDENTITY helps us align our spending plan with our values. It also helps us recognize our own responsibility to manage our financial resources and gives us the freedom to act based on what is important rather than react to the apparently urgent.

PURPOSE defines what it is we want to do with our money.

ORDER provides system to money management and clarifies the role of money as servant and not master.

CONCENTRATION enables us to channel our resources to meet specific goals.

INTEGRITY gives us the power to avoid impulse buying and unimportant expenditures. In any given moment, it empowers us to use our resources in harmony with our values.

HARMONY provides for the balanced allocation of resources and for a balance between the time spent on the acquisition of money and other goals in our lives.

And PROGRESSION empowers us to be constantly building our resources and our ability to manage them well.

The major Quadrant II strategies apply to money management as well. Your role as a financial manager can either be identified as one of the seven roles you listed earlier or included as part of one of them, such as home manager or family head. In that role, you can write a **financial mission statement** that will do for your money management what your personal mission statement has done for your management of time. This statement would reflect what you want to do with your money and how you want to do it. **It should be in harmony with your personal mission statement**, identifying your financial values and the resources you need to accomplish what is **really important** to you.

I am aware of one situation in which a woman married, and together with her husband, immediately began to focus on earning money. She was an intelligent, capable woman and, with their two incomes, they were able to get into a large, beautiful home and purchase expensive cars and recreational vehicles. Before long, she gave birth to a son. This woman was delighted and she deeply wanted to be home with him as a full time mother. But by this time, she and her husband had locked themselves into financial obligations and a lifestyle that made it almost impossible for her to quit work. As that child took his first steps and said his first words for someone else, she found herself living with constant frustration and deep pain.

As you analyze your money-making potential, be sure to look at money for what it is—a resource to help you reach your most important goals. Remember that money should be the servant, not the master.

Your financial mission statement might address questions such as:

- What income range do I want to achieve?
- How am I going to achieve that level of income?
- What degree of financial security do I want to achieve?
- What lifestyle parameters do I want to set?
- What are my investment guidelines?
- What should I set aside for future needs,

        such as my children's education?
- What is my financial plan for retirement?
- Do I expect to need capital for a second career following retirement?
- Are all of these decisions in harmony with my personal mission statement?

Writing your financial mission statement enables you to face questions of impact such as which home or car to buy, which job to take, and what investments to make from a solid base.

After you write your statement, you can apply the strategy of **roles and goals** to translate your values in the area of finance into a meaningful spending plan. **Roles** can identify the categories of spending, such as purposeful spending, investments, reserves or savings, and sharing or contributions to church, charity or community welfare. **Goals** can specify your objectives in each area for the next 6 to 12 months.

As you do your overall weekly organizing, and you come to your role as a financial manager, you can refer to these mid-term roles and goals in the area of finance to determine the one, two or three things you want to do during the week to move ahead. As you do in every role, you can then transfer those goals to specific days and times during the week. Reviewing your financial roles and goals every week keeps your financial values clearly in mind and significantly increases your ability to make decisions based on the important rather than the apparently urgent. Weekly organizing provides context to your financial plans, yet is close enough to the reality of the spending moment to enable you to fairly accurately predict needs.

The ACTION CONNECTION in financial management comes as you live each day with integrity. When unplanned options come up, always ask yourself the "important" question to determine if a particular spending opportunity is more or less important than what you had planned. Usually, integrity means following through with what you planned when you organized your week. But there are exceptions. If your spouse breaks a leg and needs medical supplies or extra help, you can recognize the importance of the need and change your plan accordingly.

In the effort to manage money effectively, I have found three supporting strategies that bring valuable returns.

1. **Share responsibility.** If your financial world is interdependent, meaning a husband, wife or business partner is also involved in spending, set up your financial system so that both you and the other person have areas of responsibility. This involvement creates commitment to agreed upon goals. By making financial partners accountable to each other, the quality of financial decisions is improved. Also you and your partner will tend to be more supportive of each other if you both face some of the same challenges of money management.

2. **Keep accurate, up-to-the-moment records.** There is a vast array of record-keeping systems available from simple checkbook additions to sophisticated computer programs. The critical factor is to know where you are at all times.

3. **Record and evaluate major spending decisions in your daily journal.** Again, the journal forces you to clarify your thoughts and give precise expression to reasons behind your decisions. It also enables you to evaluate the wisdom of those decisions and to gain perspective over a period of time.

Money can be an almost overpowering restraining force or an empowering driving force in the accomplishment of what is important to you. Effective management of this valuable resource is based on the same principles and strategies that enable you to competently manage your time. Like all Quadrant II activities, it takes investment, but the returns are great.

The Final Factor

As you try to make "connections," is a busy signal all you're going to get?

Many people emerge from a perspective-expanding experience (which I hope reading this book has been for you) with a different view of themselves and a deep desire to change. But they try to take their newly-acquired knowledge right back into the same busy Quadrant I/III lifestyle where the "busy-ness" of the urgent and apparently urgent soon overpower it. The "busy signal" makes connection impossible.

The **final factor,** and the one ultimately determining factor in any situation involving change, is your own **freedom** and **ability to choose. You choose** your own lifestyle. **You choose** the changes you make. And if other people or circumstances control your life, it is because **you choose** to let them do so.

Now, I am firmly convinced of the value of perspective-changing experiences. I know that our behavior grows out of our perceptions, and whenever we try to change behavior alone, we are again acting on the level of symptoms and our success is minimal. Changing the way we see things empowers us to make quantum change possible in our lives.

But I also know that turning that possibility into reality is a **process**, not an event. You will not be a fully empowered, connected individual when you finish reading this book.

I hope that doesn't disappoint you. In this "quick-fix" world where you can walk into a store and find a book on just about anything "made easy," that may sound radical. But it is based on a timeless, self-validating principle of growth which is just as true in human development as it is in the garden. You can no more force instant growth in your life than you can grab your tomato seedling by the leaf, yank it up hard and expect it to immediately become a fully developed plant producing two-pound tomatoes.

An empowered, fully connected person is an awesome individual, the result of consistent investment and dynamic growth. And if that is the kind of person you choose to become, there will be times in the process of becoming that you will feel disconnected and lose the peace and confidence that comes from unity with self. You will, on occasion, not live true to the best within you and make withdrawals instead of deposits in your personal integrity account. There will be times when you get off target and you allow yourself to get distracted from your determined course, times when you experience frustration as you face values in conflict from within and without which force you to refine and redefine your deepest ideals.

But if **you choose** to become a connected individual, you can. And there are three specific things you can start doing right now to significantly leverage your change.

First, you can put on (and keep on) your Quadrant II glasses. Bottom line, Quadrant II time management is not a technique; it's a way of thinking. It's looking at events, activities, opportunities, relationships and choices through the lens of **importance** rather than the lens of **urgency**.

A Quadrant II lifestyle cannot be found in a technique or a tool or any other extrinsic factor; it is within us, in the very fabric of our thought. It's a lot more than how we manage our time day by day. It's how we lead our lives, and it plays out in every aspect of daily living—in our relationship with ourselves, our relationships with others, our productivity, our confidence in choice and change, and our inner peace.

Because what we do grows out of how we think, Quadrant II vision is the single greatest leverage to change. The strategies I have suggested in this book, such as weekly organizing and identifying roles and goals, are designed to reinforce that pattern of thinking.

Second, you can constantly work to strengthen the connections you have already made. You have started the process by stretching threads of awareness between your inner feelings and your daily actions. But threads do not have the strength to keep connections intact for long. You need to build cables. You strengthen your connections every time you review your mission statement and your roles and goals. You strengthen your connections each time you organize your week and set goals to move you forward. You strengthen your connections whenever you make a deposit in your personal integrity account by living true to your values and goals on a daily basis. You strengthen your connections each time you choose the important over the apparently urgent, each time you recognize the root of your frustrations and deal with the underlying disconnections. So work on those things that will strengthen the connections you already have.

And, third, and most important, you can **start right now doing your weekly organizing**. Whatever your current level of integration of the concepts discussed in this book, you can move yourself to higher levels every week by creating the moments of clarity to renew your perspective and plan its implementation.

Choose to spend 15 to 30 minutes a week connecting in Quadrant II. If you don't have a list of roles and goals, put down whatever roles you can come up with and set some specific goals to increase your leverage, such as:

- making an appointment with yourself to work on your personal mission statement.
- filling out your life planning chart (with your spouse, if you are married).
- researching various materials and supplies to set up a personal organizer (see the following Special Section for ideas).
- setting aside specific time for a renewing activity, such as walking.

If you were to organize this next week of your life around the things you knew about that were important to you and to act with integrity to actually do them, can you imagine how you would feel at the end of the week? If you did that every week for the next 52 weeks, can you visualize the positive changes you could make in your life? Can you see yourself moving into Quadrant II?

Let's look again at the characteristics mentioned in Chapter Two that a connected Quadrant II time manager tends to possess. As we do, review in your mind the **principles** we have talked about upon which these characteristics are based. Think of the **strategies** we have discussed to develop these characteristics. I suggest you note the applicable principles and strategies beside each characteristic as you go down the list. This will be a high-leverage learning activity for you, as you will be associating the specific ideas in the book in a different way than they were presented.

EFFECTIVE QUADRANT II TIME MANAGERS:

	Principles	Strategies
1. Keep their values clearly in mind		
2. Evaluate and limit activities and commitments based on fundamental values		
3. Free themselves to act rather than being acted upon		
4. Think ahead, prepare and organize		
5. Honor commitments to self and others		
6. Accurately determine the achievable		
7. Focus efforts and energy		
8. Continually increase personal capacity		
9. Are sensitive to others and communicate effectively		
10. Carefully select and use a few personalized tools		

As my lectures and seminars take me to different places, I come in contact with many individuals from various walks of life. I think the greatest human tragedy I see is people with talent and ability who have paid a tremendous price for their "success" and who are unhappy, unfulfilled people. They simply don't have the "right connections".

I believe the right connections are within reach. I know they have made a powerful difference in my own life. I have seen them make a powerful difference in the lives of hundreds of others. I know they are based on timeless, self-validating and empowering principles. And I know, as Emerson once observed, "Nothing can bring you peace but yourself. Nothing can bring you peace but a triumph of principles."

Your Quadrant II Time Management Tools

*Effective Quadrant II time managers
"carefully select and use a few personalized tools."*

Although we have demonstrated the use of the Weekly Worksheet, we have not dealt extensively with other specific tools to help you manage your time from Quadrant II. Because Quadrant II is a way of thinking, the most important criterion of any tool is that it reinforces your Quadrant II mind set.

The market is flooded with a wide variety of "planners" and time management materials, most of which are Quadrant I/III organizing tools. This can be confusing if you have not yet incorporated the MacGyver Factor into your life.

But if you have the MacGyver mentality, if you understand a few key **principles,** you can readily select or design the tools that will provide maximum facilitation of your efforts to be true to the best within you, to act with purpose, to retain the context of vision as you plan, to keep track of information in a simple and orderly way, and to stay in Quadrant II.

The first and most important principle to keep in mind is CONTEXT. Most planners focus on daily planning and future appointments. **The keystone to Quadrant II time management is the weekly organizing process** because it provides context in three vital ways:

1. *It enables you to plan the week in the overall context of what is most important to you. As you review your chosen roles, you automatically associate them with phrases and ideas from your personal mission statement and you refocus on your deepest values. What you plan to do is deeply connected to what you really want to be and to do.*

2. *It provides balance as you see each role in the context of all roles. You do not get lost in the apparent urgency of the demands of one particular role to the exclusion of other important roles in your life.*

3. *It helps you see each day in the larger context of the week. To focus your planning on the week rather than the day frees you from the pressure of feeling you have to do everything "today." If you have a critical project due on Friday, you can enjoy Monday and Tuesday, knowing you have time scheduled on Wednesday to get it done.*

There is no factor more vital to successful Quadrant II time management than weekly organizing. You need to have some weekly organizing tool, such as the Weekly Worksheet, to encourage that mental process.

*The second important principle is ORGANIZATION. Many tools on the market are designed to organize key information chronologically, alphabetically, or in some other seemingly logical way. But the most effective Quadrant II tools are those that organize key information by **roles**.*

An organizing tool set up with dividers that correspond to each of your role areas provides a natural and meaningful place for information to go. It constantly reinforces your focus in addition to keeping information organized and making retrieval quick and easy. Locating a particular piece of information becomes a function of associating it with a role rather than searching through dates and alphabets. And when the information is no longer immediately useful, it can be transferred to a file (which will usually be set up by subject rather than chronology).

For example, one of your role areas might be "Individual-Personal Development." Under that area in your organizer, you might include:

- *your personal mission statement*
- *your current yearly goals*
- *an exercise chart to record your progress*
- *a "perhaps" list for ideas of things you might want to incorporate as goals in this role*
- *personal notes*
- *a daily log or personal journal*

If you identified one of your roles as that of "Father" or "Mother," your corresponding organizer section might include:

- *birthday and gift ideas*
- *clothing sizes for family members*
- *personal goals your children are working on*
- *parenting improvement goals*
- *your children's school class schedules*
- *items of concern about each child you want to discuss with your spouse*
- *a "perhaps" list for ideas you might want to incorporate in this role*

When you organize by roles, you basically design your own organization. Your tool becomes the extension and support of your own mental processes rather than a "system" designed by someone else to which you have to adapt.

And this brings me to the third important principle—PERSONALIZATION. Whatever tool you use needs to be **yours.** You need to have the freedom to include, exclude, delete, change, and design what meets your needs.

You may find there are things other than key role information that you want to add to your basic organizer, such as:

- *a calendar to record future commitments and appointments*
- *financial information*
- *names and addresses (I even list these by*

roles rather than alphabetically)
- *a separate "context" section for your mission statement and yearly goals*
- *a separate section for your personal journal*
- *other supportive information*

The Covey Leadership Center and some major suppliers provide a basic tool as well as a wide variety of forms and options which allow you great flexibility in putting together what will work for you. Whatever you choose should reinforce what you are trying to do, fit into your lifestyle, and be comfortable for you to work with.

Now, if you have not yet selected a basic tool that incorporates these three principles, I strongly recommend that you try the Seven Habits Organizer that I helped design. (Well, what did you expect me to recommend?) The Weekly Worksheet used in this book is taken from that Personal Leadership System.

For information on the Seven Habits Organizer Personal Leadership System and other products and programs, contact:

Covey Leadership Center
Jamestown Square
Provo, Utah 84604
1-800-255-0777

Index

Index